THE SYMPOSIUM OF PLATO

The
Symposium
of Plato

Translated by Suzy Q Groden

Edited by John A. Brentlinger

Drawings by Leonard Baskin

The University of Massachusetts Press

Library of Congress Catalog
Card Number 79–103478

Set in Janson types and
printed in the United States of America
by Connecticut Printers, Inc.

Designed by Richard Hendel

This book is dedicated to Ann Brentlinger and Lillian Groden

Contents

INTRODUCTION:
The Cycle of Becoming in the *Symposium*   1

Translator's Preface   32

The *Symposium* of Plato   37

AFTERWORD: The Nature of Love   113

The Cycle of Becoming
in the *Symposium*

I

The *Symposium* is organized around a central theme or motif which appears and reappears on many levels and in many contexts: in the religious occasion during which the banquet occurs; in the lives of particular characters; in the political and historical situation of Athens during the period which separates the actual banquet from the narration of the story by Apollodorus; in the series of speeches itself; and in the speech of Socrates. This is the theme of a cyclic process of birth, struggle, death and rebirth—perpetual γένεσις. The scene portrayed in the *Symposium* is at once a celebration of this cycle, an exemplification of it, and an occasion of reflection upon it.

Dionysus is the presiding god of the banquet. The banquet is a "drinking-together" in honor of this god, on the occasion of his festival at which the tragedian Agathon won his first contest. The person of Dionysus embodied the life-giving forces of nature; his worship centered around the yearly cycle of birth, death, and vernal rebirth, and his cult celebrated or mourned the transformations of his being which symbolized this cycle. Out of the cult grew tragedy and comedy as distinct art forms, which even in Plato's time, however, were essentially part of a religious festival dedicated to the god, presided over by his priests, acted by his "artists" (Διονύσου τεχνῖται). Eros, too, according to Socrates, personifies the movements of the same struggle: it is his nature as a daemon to pass from heaven to earth and back again perpetually, as a principle of desire whose hold on life and its goods is constantly broken due to his natural "barrenness" (πενία) and regained again by virtue of a flow of vigor and life, yet again to be lost. Dionysus, Eros, and Apollo together embody the full dimensions of the conception of life to be found in the *Symposium*. Dionysus is a young god, passionate and full of hope, whose mysteries are bound up with the cycle of life and whose symbolic death at the year's end is mitigated only by the renewal of life to come. He is balanced, in Plato's view, by Apollo, who personifies the calm of reason and the possibility of a different type of death. We hear little of Apollo in the *Symposium*, but what we do hear is significant: at the end of the party, when all others fall into a sleep symbolizing the death of mortal efforts, Socrates and his follower Aristodemus go to wash at the Lyceum, which was adjacent to the temple of Apollo and is named after him (Λύκειος being an epithet of Apollo). The true Apollonian dialogue is the *Phaedo*, from which the *Symposium* should never be separated; there Eros is a striving *for* death, and the dimension of eternity and immortality is seen to dominate a process which, while identical with the Eros of the *Symposium*, is yet viewed from the perspective of its *finale* rather than in its origin. Dionysus and Apollo thus personify two poles, the γένεσις and the τέλος of the movement of Eros.

The axis of the *Symposium*, the plot or sequence of events which draws together the characters, whether speakers or listeners, is of course the series of speeches in praise of love. However notwithstanding the fact that the main impulse underlying the dialogue is theoretical or reflective, other elements are prominent in the background which set off the speeches in their context in life and thus heighten their importance by giving them a key role in this context. One such factor is the victory of Agathon two days before in his first contest as a tragic poet—and more generally the religious context of the banquet. A second is the personal careers of the characters, most notably Alcibiades, but also others such as Agathon, Phaedrus, Eryximachus, and Glaucon (who is literally in the background as a listener). A third such factor is the political dimension, and particularly the career of Athens during this period.

First, then, the religious background. Agathon, whose name puns with "good" (ἀγαθός; a pun made by Socrates early in the dialogue, which adumbrates one basic question of the dialogue—"What is the proper object of love?" "What should be one's ἀγαθός?"), is the host of the banquet and the object of the celebration. Socrates uses adjectives suggesting the sun (and thus the Good) when he speaks of his wisdom, ". . . [it] glistens and is so full and generous. It radiated brilliantly from your youth and came to light just the other day, for a witness of more than thirty thousand Greeks!" (175E). Alcibiades, when he enters the scene, bellows "Agathon! Agathon!" and proceeds to crown with ribbons what he calls ". . . the head of the wisest and most beautiful . . ." (212E). It is youth at its finest, brilliantly showing forth in life's struggles, which attracts this adulation and motivates the gathering. Socrates' praise, however, is ironic; he mockingly adopts the attitude of the multitude—as Agathon himself realizes—but will shed it later on to put this reputation to the test. (Socrates avoided the celebration of the day before "because of the crowd," which attests to his wishing to dissociate himself from the popular response to Agathon.) Clearly Agathon and Socrates are the dramatic protagonists of this work, and clearly Plato wished his reader to note the deep contrast between Agathon's position of eminence at the time of the banquet, where all view him as an "adorable genius," and the reality, which is that he talks without knowing what he says (201B) and is thus the opposite of wise, yet possesses potentiality for greatness.

Agathon's youth and beauty, creative energy, his "calling" as a poet, make him an exemplary follower of Dionysus—or perhaps it would be closer to Plato's intentions if we saw him as symbolizing the same forces which the god himself represents. Alcibiades compares Socrates to the sileni and satyrs who follow in the train of Dionysus; a silenus is an older "teacher" satyr, and we know of statues in which Dionysus appears as a child in the company of such a satyr who is his παιδαγωγός, just as, according to Alcibiades, the satyric Socrates, wearing the mask of a prospective lover, seeks out young men to be their teacher. Further parallels are suggested when one considers that Agathon's γένεσις as a tragic poet is being celebrated—with much emphasis on his youth—at the festival dedicated to the γένεσις of Dionysus. Let us recall further the excellent point made by Helen Bacon,[1] namely that Plato presents Agathon and Socrates as contestants in their speeches on love; that they jibe with one another about their respective wisdom, and that Agathon suggests that they "go to court" about who is wiser ". . . and Dionysus shall be our judge." In the light of these points it appears that Plato is arranging the sequence of dramatic events to mirror the events which are celebrated by the Dionysian cult; these are, roughly, three: the birth and marriage of the god; an ἀγών or contest and defeat followed by death or sleep; and his resurrection beginning a new year. In the *Symposium* the dramatic action covers a four-day period: first is the day on which Agathon won his victory; second, the day of sacrifice and drunkenness in homage to Dionysus (this observance causing the characters to complain of hangovers on the third day); third, the drinking party at the house of Agathon, at which the speeches are made and Socrates and Agathon have a "poetic" contest. This day ends in a drunken revel only when all have finally passed into sleep; in this context Socrates, rising to begin the fourth day with a bath at the Lyceum, is like a risen god among the debris of spent mortality. He, it appears, and not Agathon, is the victor and the true symbol of Dionysus.

The actual dramatic date of the *Symposium* is not the time of the banquet, of course (that is, 416) but about ten years later; we as readers observe Apollodorus ("gift of Apollo") telling the story, which he learned from Aristodemus, to an unidentified group characterized only as "friends of the rich." This event too occurs on a "third day," for "the day before yesterday" Apollodorus had met Glaucon out walking and honored *his* request to hear "the speeches in praise of love." What is the point of such a complex introduc-

1. For her excellent article, "Socrates Crowned," see *The Virginia Quarterly Review*, v (1959), 415–430.

tion? As Helen Bacon points out, we are forced to view the later careers of the characters as a sequel to the banquet itself; ten years have passed, and we along with Glaucon and Apollodorus can observe how the mettle of their characters, the value of their aspirations[2]—their loves—have withstood the test of time.

Here is a movement which also mirrors the cycle in the Dionysian rite—the "year" which at the time of the banquet discovers all present to be enjoying great personal and collective prosperity has run its course, and before us we find nothing but examples of folly: Agathon has fled the democracy to the court of Archelaus, an infamous tyrant, who, driven mad by ambition, slew his cousin, uncle, and father to gain a throne, and later was assassinated himself by his lover (the career of this man, and the admiration his "courage" evoked from the followers of Gorgias, with whom Agathon must be included, are discussed in the *Gorgias* 47Aff; for a hint of Agathon's connection with Gorgias, see *Symposium* 198c); Alcibiades has fulfilled the course of his incredible career as traitor and adventurer; Phaedrus and Eryximachus have been exiled, accused of participation with Alcibiades in the scandalous mutilations of many of the stone Hermae in Athens; of the remainder only Aristophanes and Socrates (a clown and a satyr!) are known to be still alive and in Athens. This spectacle of young, talented aristocrats ruined by the very energy and power which might have brought them greatness gives to the question of love—the proper character of man's aspirations—a tremendous urgency and relevance. Glaucon and Apollodorus—boys at the time of the banquet, now entering manhood—suggest the beginnings of a new generation and a new hope, but only—Plato seems to say—on condition that they learn more of love than did those at Agathon's house that night in 416.

Due to the importance of Alcibiades' role in the Peloponnesian War we are brought onto still another level of the cycle of tri-

---

2. Depending on the context 'aspiration' or 'desire' may be a better English equivalent of ἔρως than 'love.'

umph and defeat, that of Athens herself. When Agathon won his
first victory Athens was likewise at the peak of her power, and
preparing to extend her empire to Italy and even beyond. The
Syracusan invasion and its disastrous consequences, as Thucydides
made clear, was an inevitable result of the Periclean imperialism;
peace had become an impossibility for the Athenians, and Alcibiades was able to argue, in his speech favoring the invasion, that the
glory of the Athenians lay in their despising peace, and that for
better or worse they must live up to their character as imperialists:
". . . we cannot fix the exact point at which our empire shall stop;
we have reached a position in which we must not be content at re-
taining but must scheme to extend it, for, if we cease to rule others,
we are in danger of being ruled ourselves."[3] The condition of
Athens at that time, when Plato was eleven years old, her downfall,
and the tremendous personal and public losses incurred, remained
long in his thoughts; we find in the dialogues much bitter criticism
of the Periclean policies, and above all an uncompromising con-
demnation, in the *Republic*, of democracy as the state of "appetite," a society in which stupidity and cowardice are combined
with unlimited desire for wealth. By the time of Apollodorus' telling of the story the political ruin of Athens is complete, and we are
thus exposed to the vast social and political dimensions of mis-
guided Eros. The mention of Glaucon, in the opening remarks of
the *Symposium*, serves further to strengthen the political implications of the discourses on love, and suggests the possibility of social
rebirth in the philosophical state. For we next meet Glaucon, of
course, in the *Republic*,[4] where he and Socrates—now companions

3. *Thucydides*, Book VI, 18, 18.
4. The presence of Glaucon as hearer of the "discourse on love" two
days before suggests that Plato makes little attempt to adhere strictly to
historical chronology in dramatically "placing" the dialogues. This, of
course, breaks down an assumption which Taylor has made popular. On
Taylor's view the dramatic date of the *Republic* is 422–421, that of the
Symposium 416. But in the *Symposium* we read that Glaucon was a boy
(παῖς) in 416, thus obviously much younger than in the *Republic*. On
the other hand, Socrates' remarks about old age in the *Republic* could

—are attending a different festival, that of Bendis the Thracian Artemis, goddess of hunting and midwifery, the two most common Platonic metaphors for dialectic inquiry.

II

The speeches of the *Symposium* introduce still another level in this Dionysian drama, the level of reflection attempting to comprehend the nature of love. They begin with the discourse of Phaedrus, and the series contains altogether eight parts divided into two principal sequences.[5]

FIRST SEQUENCE	SECOND SEQUENCE
(*The Effects of Love*)	(*Love's Nature and Effects*)
Phaedrus	Agathon
Pausanias	Agathon and Socrates
Eryximachus	Socrates
Aristophanes	Alcibiades

The two sequences are clearly marked off from one another, first by a dramatic interlude, second when Agathon criticizes the first group as a whole for failing to discuss the nature of Eros and for concentrating on its effects on man. This is a vague though familiar point in Plato. He has claimed in several other dialogues that it is impossible to know anything *about* an object unless one first knows *what* it is—its nature or essence (for example *Meno* 71B, *Republic* 354B). And in the *Phaedrus* it is claimed that discourses are clearer and more orderly if they begin with a definition of their

---

hardly have been made—as Taylor points out—by a man over 60, and thus dramatically, not after 416 or so. The conclusion is simply that there is some lack of historical coherence here in the dating; Plato is willing to adapt the ages and circumstances of his characters to fit dramatic and philosophical purposes.

5. I am indebted to Professor Meyer W. Isenberg for some of the basic ideas in this sequence. See his "The Order of the Discourse in Plato's Symposium" (Ph.D. Dissertation; University of Chicago, 1946).

subject, so that at the least one's assumptions concerning the nature of the subject are made explicit (265D). In Socrates' speech in the *Symposium* we see that by an account of the nature of love Plato means a description which classifies love (as a kind of object-directed desire) and proceeds from this to characterize and relate the objects desired (the Good, immortality, happiness, fame, sexual pleasure, and so on). Love's "effects," then, are the actions and pursuits of men, in carrying out their love and desire for "immortal possession of the Good."

Though Agathon calls for an account of love's nature he botches it terribly, for he identifies love (as Plato sees it, impossible without desire) with a complete and perfect state of being (which thus lacks desire). In the first four discourses the failure to discuss love's nature leads—as we shall see—to the satirical laughter of Aristophanes. Phaedrus appears to assume, without explicit statement, that love is sexual attraction of one person for another aroused by beauty, and devotes his speech to the elevating actions that love may cause. In the speeches of Pausanias and Eryximachus more sophisticated and complex accounts of love's effects are given, but love's nature is further obscured, to the point that, for Eryximachus, the most perfect love is between opposites, objects which on the psychological level *hate* (ἔχθω 186D) one another!

In Phaedrus' discourse love is assumed to be sexual desire aroused in the presence of beauty. Love's great power consists in causing those who wish to be loved to be beautiful, that is, to avoid ugly and shameful deeds and to perform beautiful actions in order to win the favor of a beloved. The actions ideally suited for this effect are heroic deeds, in which danger and sacrifice and—as love's most perfect expression—death are undergone as homage to the beloved. Thus the value of love, according to Phaedrus, is in causing men to do good in order to excite the admiration of a beloved. This highly romantic, aristocratic conception, like all of the theories of love in the *Symposium*, reflects a certain point of view of the speaker. In Phaedrus the point of view is that of the littérateur, as he refers continually to the poets and draws all of his information and examples from their stories. Love, it seems, is the cause of those actions it is the province of literature to depict and celebrate. Phaedrus, himself, were he alive today, would be a scholar or critic of literature. Indeed he cannot refrain from entering into a critical dispute with Aeschylus over how to best construe the relationship between Patroclus and Achilles! Also, it is to Phaedrus that all of the other speakers address their speeches, as he has noticed and complained of the lack of any encomium made to Eros, in all the works of poets up to his day.

Has Phaedrus' speech a function other than as a bland introduction to the speeches which follow? If Plato has chosen the speakers with some attention to the point of view they bring to the subject, it is probably because he thinks each point of view in some way contributes to an understanding of love. In support of this is the fact that there are elements in Socrates' speech corresponding to each of the previous speeches. The most direct connection with Phaedrus' speech is Socrates' explanation of the great deeds of Alcestis and Achilles (208D), which had provided Phaedrus with a large part of his evidence for the view that love is the cause of "ambition for noble deeds" (178D). Phaedrus and Socrates agree that the primary value of love consists in its causing high and noble actions. Perhaps Plato would say, then, that they agree, at least in part, on the sort of *effects* love has on men. Their great difference lies in an area Phaedrus does not even discuss: the "nature" of love, that is, the aspirations and state of mind of a truly heroic lover.

Pausanias takes over Phaedrus' account, but adds new complexity by considering the social and political effects of love. The sexual response to beauty is, from this social standpoint, a merely natural fact which is potentially good or bad depending on the way it is directed. Laws or norms or customs (νόμοι) are patterns to which love behavior must be related if social values are not to be destroyed by "heroic deeds." Thus arises the concepts of the utility and harmfulness of actions relative to their consequences for the social fabric. Phaedrus had completely ignored the ethical dimension of love-behavior, assuming that it is always "beautiful and noble" (καλός), as it appears, no doubt, in the eyes of a foolish and romantic young man being seduced by an admired elder. But as Pausanias remarks at the beginning of his discourse, actions viewed apart from the context of motives and consequences are neither noble nor ignoble. Heroism judged aesthetically is for storybooks —in life we examine the consequences of deeds, and the true heroes are those who achieve some excellent result. Thus Pausanias is led to distinguish a good and bad—a heavenly and earthly—love, depending on whether passion is channeled in ways which further or destroy human happiness.

Generally, Pausanias appears to hold that happiness has two components: bodily pleasure and cultivation of the mind. The difficulty is to engineer society so that both may be realized in the same persons. Pausanias develops a rather contorted theory of laws in his speech. He rejects heterosexual love as manifestly degrading —it belongs to "earthly" love. Thus he assumes that women are mentally too low either to learn from or to educate; since only physical love is possible with women, heterosexual relations are "earthly" or "common." But Pausanias is also concerned that male homosexuality be regulated lest relationships between men and boys degenerate to a merely sensual level. The "double laws" of Athens provide the clue he wishes, through the paradox that they encourage the lover yet restrain and discourage the beloved: those with purely carnal motives are presumably restrained, and only lovers with patience and concern for the spiritual well-being of the beloved are at last rewarded with his favors. The result is a social system based on a kind of barter and exchange of physical and spiritual values.[6] An older man, who is virtuous and wise, and a boy physically in his prime but in need of wisdom and virtue, are the ideal lovers. For each has what the other needs. This, according to Pausanias, is a perfect social arrangement; bodily needs are satisfied

6. That this is exactly Plato's opinion of Pausanias' theory is shown when we learn of Alcibiades' attempt to pull off this bargain with Socrates. Socrates tells him: "you are trying to trade bronze for gold" (219A).

and yet at the same time turned to a socially productive end—that of education and the creation in the state of permanent relationships among men.

The speech of Eryximachus brings to bear on the problem of love still a third perspective—that of natural science. It was characteristic of Greek physics in Socrates' time—as it is, to a lesser extent, of modern physics as well—to explain the behavior of all physical bodies in terms of the properties of simple, elemental bodies, and certain very general types of interaction and change. Eryximachus' hypothesis is an original synthesis of the at that time very respectable results of Empedoclean and Heracleitean cosmology, and Pythagorean medical theory. The first taught that Eros was a fundamental natural force of attraction between bodies; the second that the elements which compose nature are opposite qualities which, when balanced in a state of equilibrium, give a relative unity, stability and thus harmony to the larger whole of which they are parts. Pythagorean medical theory—with which Eryximachus begins, since he is a physician—taught, similarly, that the body's well-being or health—its wholeness as an organism—rested on the existence of an equal balance between its elemental components, for example dry and moist, hot and cold, bitter and sweet. Eryximachus envisions nature as a vast field of such qualities, generating forces by virtue of their qualitative opposition, while order, regularity, and the stability which exist in the "pockets" of nature we call "things" or "objects" are due to a balance or harmony among the opposites. Within this larger, cosmic outlook, the distinctions of Pausanias hold good, however: there is a dual nature to love, that is a good and bad love, as for example in the health and disease of the body. Health is, as Heracleitus would put it, a unity of what is at variance with itself. Disease and all things bad, on the other hand, are caused by an excess of one of the opposites, which disrupts the prevailing harmony. The good, then, is a harmony of opposites; the bad a coming-together of similars. How does this apply to human love? Eryximachus gives a hint at the beginning of his speech: there he remarks to Pausanias that although his speech started off well it had a lame ending, and *he* will bring it to a proper close. And he does indeed complete Pausanias' theory—by generalizing it. For the view that love should hold between the old, wise and good, and ignorant and unformed youths is based upon their differences from one another. Each has what the other lacks and needs. Therefore it can be viewed as a special case of the general theory that love and harmony result from the coming together of opposites. A general corollary of Eryximachus' science of love, for social theory, is that harmony will exist only among complementary personality types!

Aristophanes, as presented in the *Symposium*, is second only to Socrates in his grasp of the mysteries of love. Indeed he dramatically fulfills a role in relation to the first three speeches which in other dialogues belongs peculiarly to the Socratic art of question and answer—that of a wise critic, that is, one who sees the deficiency in another's opinion and is able to locate precisely the point of error, but who pleads ignorance, in his turn, and refuses to make a positive contribution. It is essential in understanding the *Symposium* to grasp this point, namely the similarity between the comic poet and the dialectician: both are adept at exposing—to the general amusement—the pretensions of others. The similarity stops on this negative side; it is also a part of dialectic to offer positive theories and ideas, to which it turns about to play the role of critic again. The comic poet, however, is not a theoretician; insofar as his criticisms of others have any positive foundations they are those of common sense or the conservative traditions of society.

The first sign of Aristophanes' restiveness occurs after Pausanias' speech, where we find he has the hiccups. He got them during the speech itself. At this point the dialogue begins to get funny and Plato's contempt for Greek physics takes over. As George Kimball Plochmann has pointed out,[7] they cannot be caused by overdrink-

---

7. In "Hiccups and Hangovers in the Symposium," *Bucknell Review*, XI (1963), 1–18, a stimulating discussion of some of the "minor" dramatic occurrences in the dialogue.

ing, for the company has agreed to be moderate. However they are due to a surfeit of *something*, and what more likely candidate than the speeches themselves! To appreciate Plato's artistry here we must dramatize the scene to ourselves: imagine hiccups growing louder and more frequent in the latter part of Pausanias' speech, and then while Eryximachus unveils his cosmic scheme, the various attempts at a cure: Aristophanes holding his breath, reddening to the point of explosion, the gasping for air followed by more and louder hiccups; gargling wine, but still more hiccups; finally, he tickles his nose with a feather, sneezes and blows—which should coincide with the climax of Eryximachus' speech (188D)—and achieves success. This counterpoint of lugubrious theorizing and clowning should be staged to be appreciated—it is worthy of Molière or indeed Aristophanes himself.

A further comic implication of the hiccups episode is the sample it provides of Eryximachus' art of applying harmony to the body. Aristophanes had asked Eryximachus either to cure his hiccups or to speak in his place, and the latter, characteristically, will do both ('Eryximachus' *means* belch-fighter). Thus he at once gives us a demonstration of his medical art, and sets himself up, with a long and serious face, for the fantastic scene to follow. We have already mentioned the three cures Aristophanes tried at the doctor's suggestion. The first was to hold the breath, which follows the principle of harmony of opposites—that is, outer constraint applied to violent inner motion—but it failed to work. What did work—the last alternative—was the sneezing, that is, violent inner motion applied to violent inner motion. Aristophanes wondered if the harmony of the body requires these "noises and titilations"; for evidently harmony was restored by the coming together of similars. This result delights Aristophanes greatly, for he is about to present a very different theory of human nature, according to which not opposites but similars attract and fall in love. (Aristophanes points out that his view is quite different from that of Eryximachus and Pausanias: 189C, and again at 193D.)

In an earlier age, according to Aristophanes' natural history, man lived a happier existence; there were three sexes then: a male-male sex, descended from the sun; a female-female, born from earth; and an androgynous sex, born from the moon—since the moon shares in both light and earth. Man's happiness lay in his power, which was very great; he was an eight-limbed, two-faced creature who could move across the earth with great speed, like a tumbling acrobat. But due to this power the original men sinned the sin of pride and attacked heaven. The gods were at a loss; they did not wish to annihilate humanity, for then no one would pay them honor. Presently, Zeus, according to Aristophanes, put his wits together and conceived the solution; he would slice all men in half, and thus they would be at once chastened and weakened, and also doubled in number, so that sacrifices would increase also in the same proportion. However, to man the event was a trauma. Apollo smoothed and rounded us as best he could, tying off the skin at the navel and setting the head around; but mankind was and is still awkward and forlorn, the victim of an agonizing shock. What, then, is love? It is the unconscious and all-powerful desire to be restored to one's primordial other half. This desire is the source of the great significance of the sexual act, yet we hardly, or at least only vaguely, grasp this.

This very funny and ingenious speech functions in the dialogue in two principal ways. First as an attack on Eryximachus, Aristophanes offers the alternative that similars and not opposites are proper lovers. For as he repeatedly says, people seek those *like themselves* in sex (192A: τὸ ὅμοιον αὑτοῖς ἀσπαζόμενοι. 192B: ἀεὶ τὸ συγγενὲς ἀσπαζόμενος). This too, I think, is what he is suggesting in his cryptic claim to be giving a very different speech from Eryximachus (193D, 189C). Yet this is not with speculative intentions; his purpose is surely parody.[8] His alternative serves, by stark contrast, to point up the limitations of any attempt to understand hu-

---

8. For the suggestion that Aristophanes' speech parodies a physicalistic account of human behavior—and for many other insights into the workings of the *Symposium*—I am indebted to Professor Robert S. Brumbaugh, with whom I studied the *Symposium* as a student. For a short account by him of the *Symposium* see *Plato for the Modern Age* (New York: Crowell Collier, 1963), pp. 83–85.

man behavior in terms of a simple, fixed pattern or rule. Aristophanes, as we know from *The Clouds,* is a plausible opponent of the new physical science. And through him, I suggest, Plato is leveling an attack on materialistic theories of human nature. Aristophanes' puppet-like creatures, who automatically embrace their "likes," are caricatures of men when understood as dominated by a crudely mechanistic principle of attraction or repulsion.

Plato's main objection to the "physics" of such thinkers as Empedocles, Anaximander, and Anaxagoras, is that they ignore the "value-seeking" dimension of man; and, according to him, it is impossible for a materialistic philosophy to do otherwise. The point is made explicit by Socrates later in the *Symposium,* when he says:

> Whereas a person might make up a story . . . that those who seek after the other halves of themselves are loving, my own account describes love as being neither of the half nor of the whole, unless it should chance, my friend, to be something good. . . . (205E)

A clearer statement of Plato's view occurs in the *Phaedo,* where Socrates is discussing the philosophy of Anaxagoras (97c). Socrates criticizes Anaxagoras for failing to give purposive or teleological explanations in which the mind acts in order to bring about good. Rather, he says, Anaxagoras appeals only to physical causes. He would try to explain actions by reference to the movements of our bones and muscles and sinews, rather than our convictions concerning what is right; or explain speech by wind and air and hearing rather than by reference to the purposes or aims of the speakers. Physical causes, Socrates says, are necessary but not sufficient to explain our actions (99A), which are also caused by the mind and involve consideration of what is best (99B). To ignore the mind (and thus a man's desire for goodness) is to consider only a part of human nature; that Aristophanes' men should be *half-men* is a beautiful touch, where their mindlessness and their lack of a conception of goodness or beauty is metaphorically represented.

A second function of Aristophanes' speech is to restore desire, and particularly sexual desire, to its proper importance. Sexuality had figured importantly in Phaedrus' and Pausanias' speeches, but it was kept in the background. All the easier, then, for Phaedrus to romanticize it, to the extent that only heroes seem capable of real love; and for Pausanias to restrict allowed love to pairs of wise and older men and attractive young boys. Both allow only a select group an acceptable form of love, and both narrowly restrict the sort of actions which can count as legitimate expressions even of sexual love.

Moreover the role of desire becomes more problematic as the speeches develop. Pausanias wishes to show how sexual relationships (neither good nor bad in themselves) can be engineered so as to produce good consequences—education of (some of) the young. But he pairs off citizens without regard for desire and the character of its object. He presupposes that his ideal lover, the wise and virtuous older man, is motivated by desire, yet if he desires wisdom and virtue why does he love the neither wise nor good (that is young boys)? At this point one may guess that the hiccups begin! Again, consider the beloved. If he does not desire the older man, how can he love? But if he does love the older, then it must be because he desires wisdom and virtue, and not the pleasures of sex. But if that were so, would not the youth be proving himself better than the man who is to teach him wisdom and virtue? Plato does not raise these points in the *Symposium*—they are, as it were, embodied in the hiccups—but we may guess that they were on his mind, because, first, a similar set of paradoxes is discussed in an earlier dialogue, the *Lysis* (215cff), in a consideration of a similar problem—whether opposite can be friend to opposite. There the view is rejected on the ground that the just and the unjust, the temperate and the intemperate, cannot be friends. Though the "opposition" in the present case is not as great as that, it is clear that Plato's attitude would be the same. For when Alcibiades broaches such a relationship with Socrates, he is turned down flat. If a man gets to the point of being an educator, Plato holds, his interest in his students is not physical. His concern is for the virtues of character and the pleasures of conversation.

A new problem for the relation of desire to love is raised by

Eryximachus' theory. The most opposite things, according to him, are most hostile to one another (186D), yet love, at least the higher, heavenly love, exists only among opposites which have been balanced or harmonized. This seems to eliminate desire as a factor in love. The tendencies of lovers are opposed, and their harmony is a result of the power of each to counteract and balance the tendencies of the other. Harmony is thus a product of tension. Insofar as their relationship can be said to be based upon common interests, however, the theory of Eryximachus no longer applies.

As a person who devotes half his time to Dionysus, and half to Aphrodite (177E), Aristophanes would understandably wish to loose all his arrows at such theories. If love is anything it is a desire for the loved object. Yet his speech does not replace the preceding ones with a new theory; his discourse is myth because what he fights is also myth, and we are left with only the common truism that love is a sense of need expressed by an urgent sexuality. The true effect of his speech is to give the deathblow—in the form of a comic dance—to the attempts to understand love-behavior without a comprehensive theory of human desire. The Dionysian cycle has led from birth—Phaedrus is called the father of the argument (177D)—to pretended triumph to death of the argument. We must turn now to its rebirth in the discourse of Agathon.

In the interlude which separates the two sequences of discourses, Agathon and Socrates again take up their bantering, as we find ourselves preparing for the contest between them. We have already indicated that the adored Agathon, who shone like the sun two days before, is to be tested by Socrates for his true wisdom. The ground is prepared when they distinguish between Agathon performing before "many fools" or before "a few men of wit." Socrates wonders whether Agathon is really going to treat the present company to a special brand of wisdom, and if he would do things before the one group which would shame him before the other. Thus we have a retrial of Agathon, yet now before a few connoisseurs.

Agathon's thesis concerning Eros is, first, that he is the most beautiful of gods, second, that he is virtuous. He is beautiful because young, delicate, pliant, and brightly colored. Concerning his virtue, he is wise because a poet, and because he makes a poet of others; and in addition, temperate, courageous, and just (for example, why is he temperate? temperance is control over desire, and since love is the strongest desire he controls other desires!). In the final paragraph Agathon speaks of love's effects, in a rhetorical tour de force; the result is a hodge-podge, the actual point being that love is the cause of all good things.

Those who read Agathon's speech for its content alone—it has almost none—are naturally put off by its shallowness and consequently mystified by its position late in the series of discourses and by the tremendous applause it receives. The real point of the speech, however, lies in the *self-glorification* Agathon is able to achieve in it—in his ability to appear to speak of love while really praising himself, *his* youth, beauty, and wisdom. His words *trivially* apply to love, and by balancing on a line between clear—and thus shameful—self-praise, and clear praise of love—which would not redound to himself—he gets precisely the wanted result: a blurring of identities between himself and the god, with an effect which is, if not enlightening, at least marvelously stimulating. We may see the point more clearly from a remark in Socrates' speech: Socrates, who had also thought love to be beautiful and good, is told by Diotima: "You supposed that the beloved and not the lover was love." Agathon too equates passion with the object of passion. His youthful exuberance, a cynosure to all present, finds its highest value in the release and enjoyment of itself. Thus in his speech we have in actuality a symbol of the Dionysian spirit. Its effect on the company was great: ". . . the people who were there applauded this speech which so became the young man who had given it, as well as the god!" (198A).

It is in such terms that we must understand Socrates' interest in Agathon, his attempt to chastise and direct the vigorous talents of the man. We are reminded at once of Alcibiades, another passionate and talented young man with whom Socrates had much to do. We must now also note, however, the attraction which Socrates has for *them* (recall the half-serious jealousy Alcibiades displays when he discovers Socrates and Agathon reclining on the same couch). Both Agathon and Alcibiades touched Socrates and asked to receive "the wisdom" they so strongly desired for themselves. After Socrates, on his way to the banquet, retired onto the porch of a neighboring house to think (standing, undoubtedly, next to just such a Hermes [= 'messenger'] as Alcibiades was later supposed to have mutilated, for it was the custom to have stone Hermae on the porches of houses and temples), Agathon said: "Here, Socrates, sit by me and eat so by touching you I may partake of some of that wisdom which has come to you on the porch" (175D). This powerful image of passive but vigorous potentiality inviting impregnation—compare the *Phaedrus*' elaboration of this metaphor (276Aff)—from the older, wiser, and more virtuous is one of the central themes of the *Symposium*. And for Plato its import is wider than sexuality or education alone; rather it epitomizes his view of human life as a whole, in which the energies of the self reach for a principle of form, by which, impregnated, they may realize definite and enduring values. Love, for Plato, is an explosive force or energy of the soul which contains within it, somehow, intimations of a supreme good toward which it is directed.

There has so far been in the speeches a curious relation between the speakers themselves and the love of which they speak. On the one hand each speech has been dominated by the perspective of the speaker's occupation or special interest. For example, Phaedrus concentrates exclusively on the sort of human behavior which is heroic, and therefore particularly lends itself to poetic treatment. In this sense the discourses are expressions of self-love; the special concerns and "tastes" of the self in each case have been given the status of privileged avenues to truth. Yet there is also a sense in which the loves of the speakers have in *no* way been reflected in their discourses. For their love is shown in the love they give to some object or pursuit to which the work of their lives is devoted. If love is a cause of human action—if men toil for some one or more of the goods of life out of love—this is no small or quibbling disparity: rather, for Phaedrus—to continue this example—to say nothing of the love of letters, and of the value to man of literature, betrays a shocking ignorance of the motives which guide his life. In actuality Phaedrus cares less for *Liebestoden* than for the poetry which celebrates, purifies, and immortalizes human action. The latter is great *only* in the poetry. Part of the importance of Socrates' speech is that the love of art, of laws and politics, of science *and* sexual love, are dealt with by the same theory. There is harmony between the content of the theory and the person who creates it.

In Agathon's discourse these parallel factors—self-glorification and self-ignorance—reach a kind of climax. The content of his speech is ambiguously applicable to love and to himself; while on the other hand he attempts to identify love (and thus himself)— really nothing to Plato but promise, potentiality, great and urgent desire—with the good itself, with beauty, wisdom, and virtue! The anger and distaste with which Socrates expresses his criticism—for appearing to praise love when actually he has only put together fine phrases—is intended as a strong rebuff to Agathon; and the section of question and answer, in which it is argued that love is neither good nor beautiful, but rather a kind of desire or aspiration, continues this chastisement. Socratic question and answer, insofar as its force is negative, is a rebuke to intellectual and moral pretensions on behalf of self-knowledge. To Socrates the first part of self-knowledge is awareness of the essential "poverty" of the self—an awareness which comes only with *elenchus*. For example Plato writes in the *Sophist* of those who undergo "the art of refutation":

> But those who see this [that is, the contradictions in their opinions] grow angry with themselves and gentle toward others, and this is the way in which they are freed from their high and obstinate opinions about themselves. The process of freeing them, moreover, affords the greatest pleasure to the listeners and the most lasting benefit to him who is subjected to it. . . . We must assert that cross-questioning is the greatest and most efficacious of purifications, and that he who is not cross-questioned, even though he be the Great King, has not

been purified of the greatest taints, and is therefore uneducated and deformed in those things in which he who is to be truly happy ought to be most pure and beautiful. (*Sophist* 230B–E)

That the Socratic speech should be in dialogue form is of considerable importance; it is thus able to dramatize certain themes of the speech itself by depicting Socrates' education in love. Also, a very interesting relation is created between the speech and the rest of the dialogue. On the one hand, since the Socratic speech is demonstrably the climax of the series of discourses, and offers the Platonic account of love, it functions as a beacon which illumines all the other parts or aspects of the *Symposium:* the earlier speeches, the dramatic and historical action depicted or suggested, all motivated by a type of love, become the *data* of this discourse, the concrete material which gives meaning and relevance to its compressed and abstract statement. On the other hand, the speech fulfills a dramatic role: one of the most important lines of development in the dialogue, which reaches a peak in Alcibiades' discourse and the final scenes of the dialogue, is the increasing recognition—by those present, those told by Apollodorus, and ourselves as readers—of the personal pre-eminence of Socrates. His discourse, then, which is the "story" of his education in love, is as important as an explanation of his great personal influence on others as in its relation to the previous speeches. It is the point of convergence of the dramatic, historical, and intellectual themes of the dialogue.

Though the discourse specifically concerns Socrates' education, it is so placed dramatically as to offer the same to Agathon. The Socrates who meets Diotima for the first time is, like Agathon, engrossed in the "glories" of love. Like Agathon he worships a god— apparently a god—he believes to be all-beautiful and good. Diotima shows him, as he showed Agathon, that a more appropriate representation of love is a daemon or spirit which exists "between" the changing, mortal level of becoming, and the unchanging, immortal and divine level of being. It connects and relates these two realms. The tale of Love's birth shows that love is intermediate, a mixture, having traits common to both. Its mother was Πενία, a female principle meaning *need* or *poverty;* hence love is a form of desire. The male element in Love gives it direction and "intelligence": the father is Πόρος, which means *contrivance, resource, way* (said to be the son of Μῆτις, *craft* or *wisdom*), and allows it to be a philosopher, having constant "designs upon the Beautiful and Good." As the Socratic speech develops the personification of Eros disappears and it is viewed as a power which actuates all living things, even animals: it is a kind of *élan vital,* giving to purposive life and activity its urgent tendencies toward realization. "Loving" is generalized to include all creative activity; the object of love is generalized as "the good," and "the eternal possession of good."

The general *effect* of love is "procreation in a beautiful thing." What does this mean? Diotima explains each part separately. In beautiful things because beauty is a "symbol" of the divine, the good: "The ugly clashes with all that is divine, while beauty is in harmony with it." Mortal beings respond to beauty and are repelled by ugliness, and the former is the felt presence of good. In creation, however, or begetting, we have a "symbol" of eternal possession. All of nature teems with the creative urge; all are obsessed with the desire to procreate and rear their offspring. Why is this? Because to mortal things immortality lies in perpetual becoming, permanence in endless renewal. We constantly lose whatever we attain; we must constantly struggle to replace what is lost:

> It is in this way that everything mortal is preserved—not by
> its being utterly the same forever, like the divine, but by what
> is old and withdrawing leaving behind something else, some-
> thing new, like itself. It is by this method, Socrates, that the
> mortal partakes of immortality, she explained, in the body
> and in all other respects. It is not possible any other way.
> (208A–B)

For Plato, then, the basic human drive is desire of the Good. Since the Good is a specific object, the form of the Good, this desire could be fully realized in one specific way: by attaining possession of the Good in contemplation. Other goods and other objects of desire, however, are not merely means or instruments for the attainment of this. They may partially satisfy the Eros of man. The hierarchy of experiences Socrates describes are successively closer to the vision of the Good because they approximate in ever greater degree, the value of this vision. Their value depends on the value of the Good, but not as the value of an instrument depends on the value of its work: rather, as the value of a copy of a picture derives from the beauty of the original. Lower objects are intrinsically satisfying and good, but inferior in worth to the beauty of the Good itself.

Nor are these lower "objects" things men seek out merely to enjoy. Rather, the effects of love, the way in which "the vehemence of love" finds its way into actions is through creation—"giving birth." Being desirous of the Good, the self is moved to give form and permanence to the flux of life—to create in experience a measure of its aspiration. Life is creative struggle, man is a poet, a maker, a craftsman. The diversity of human concerns can be unified under the single theme: creating in the beautiful. Eros is human aspiration (or more strictly, the aspiration of all living things, all things having soul) in its most general aspect. Forms of eros are less general forms of human aspiration, as shown in the struggle for achievement: bodily creation (family, acts of bodily struggle in war [and Plato should have mentioned, athletics]), creation of the soul (art, teaching, laws), and finally knowledge, in which the soul acts on itself so as to bring itself into relation with a series of objects of knowledge: the beauty of bodies, souls, laws, the cosmos, and finally of the Beautiful itself. Since, for Plato, the acquisition of knowledge, and of virtue, are the same process; since a man can only come to have knowledge by raising and purifying his soul, the last (and highest) kind of achievement is a sort of self-creation, to the point where the soul attains true virtue in seeing the ultimate object of knowledge:

> Don't you realize, she asked, that only there, seeing in the way that the beautiful can be seen, can one stop giving birth to images of virtue, since one no longer holds on to images,

/ut truth, because one now grasps the truth? He is able to bring forth true virtue, and to nourish it, and hence to be a favorite of the gods, so that if any man can be immortal, it will be he. (212A)

This theory has been immensely influential in Western civilization. Its view of knowledge as man's highest activity; of human excellence as the exercise of reason; of human nature as at base the faculty of reason—became Western man's conception of himself. It also contains the seeds of our conception of the world for a long time to come. It gives a picture in which the body and soul, and society, and cosmos are like a series of nested Chinese boxes, or better, a series of organs each serving the higher organism in which it is contained. Dominating the whole is a highest being, the Good or the Beautiful, and in contemplating this entity the rational soul can find perfect and inexhaustible happiness.

Considered as a metaphysical theory of man and the world this picture is of immense aesthetic and historical interest. But we can say more than this. The *Symposium* contains great excitement for the modern reader as a living work. Its achievement in its own time raises an undying challenge: that men shall maintain a picture of themselves and the world in which all legitimate human aspiration and all legitimate forms of life are seen to function as parts of an all-embracing whole. The ideal the *Symposium* gives is the ideal of cultural wholeness. Not wholeness in the sense that the parts of society contribute functionally to the whole—this ideal, though valid, is Utopian. The wholeness we can have at any point in time is intellectual comprehension of the meaning of all forces in society, as they relate to the whole. In Plato *this* is ultimately Utopian. In Socrates' speech we have an intellectual vision in which the deepest feelings and desires are fulfilled in action and interaction and the pursuits of the mind. The ends of life complement and support one another. Yet there is a striking difference between the description of human pursuits in the speech and their description (or portrayal) through the actions and words of the characters of the dialogue. The latter are full of conflict, disagreement, frustration, and failures. They acutely and sensitively depict a set of diverse and opposing interests, yet it seems clear that part of Plato's intention is to show how they may be comprehended, and thus given meaning, in the general theory expressed in Socrates' speech.

The speech of Alcibiades, like that of Aristophanes, does not contain a positive, theoretical account, and in this sense is not a part of the series of discourses. The form of each of the two "terminal" discourses is narrative, and each through narrative brings our attention to the concrete workings of love. Each also functions critically in relation to previous discourses. Aristophanes' "natural history" of man's comic predicament, in grudging praise of love, protests the crudeness and simplicity of a materialistic view of man. Alcibiades gives a history of his tragic predicament, in grudging praise of Socrates. His drunken—and therefore sincere and true—tale of his relationship with Socrates similarly provides a return to concrete evidence of love and its effects, in the form of a case history of an actual love affair. We are undoubtedly expected to compare Alcibiades' account of the heroism of Socrates to Phaedrus' analysis of heroic deeds, and Alcibiades' attempt to barter his beauty for Socrates' goodness to Pausanias' pragmatic views of friendship. To Eryximachus' notion that opposites come together to produce a harmony we should compare the tremendous tension in the relationship between the young, wealthy, beautiful, intemperate, and foolish Alcibiades and Socrates who is in all these respects his opposite. Again, can we imagine, in accordance with Aristophanes' speech, that Socrates would fulfill his aspirations in the arms of Alcibiades? Or can we believe that the love-torn Alcibiades is beauty incarnate, and, according to Agathon, poet, virtuous, tender and supple, in youth's bloom, finding everywhere peace, harmony, and friendship, within himself and without? One effect, then, of the speech of Alcibiades, is to bring the speeches down to earth, to show their power or lack of power to interpret an extremely complex yet actual love relationship.

However Alcibiades' discourse is primarily a eulogy of Socrates, expressed, as he himself says, in the form of images (εἰκόνες). The images he uses, those of the satyr Marsyus and the pottery figures of sileni sold in bric-a-brac shops, are extremely illuminating, for the satyr is that goat-legged, fluting reveler we find pictured everywhere in Greek art, in the train of Dionysus. The satyric revels, as is well known, celebrate the coming of Dionysus and thus the renewal of the energies of life; the satyr is a lust-figure, goaded by animal desire, yet divine. This paradoxical combination of qualities ideally suits a figure which personifies the process of perpetual renewal.

Socrates, then, is a satyr—half animal, half god—a reveler, a piper, whose "songs" according to Alcibiades produce the most extraordinary effects, what we might call 'the Dionysian effect': a leaping of the heart, gushing of tears, tremblings—the inner tumult of the Corybantes ($\kappa o \rho v \beta a v \tau \iota \acute{\omega} v \tau \epsilon s$ 215E); in short what Diotima called the inner movement of desire awakened by beauty.[9] The beauty Socrates presents is the beauty of truth, the tantalizing prospect of knowledge; his song philosophic discourse. Alcibiades compares the effect to the traumatic bite of an adder:

> And yet I have the same feeling as the man who was bitten by the snake. They say he didn't want to tell anyone what that experience was like, unless they had been bitten themselves, since only such a person could understand and forgive him if he ran wild and raved in his agony. And you see, I have been bitten by a more painful thing, and in the most painful way that one can be bitten—in the heart or soul or whatever else

9. Compare A. E. Housman's description of the symptoms produced by poetry in his essay "The Name and Nature of Poetry": "Experience has taught me, when I am shaving of a morning, to keep watch over my thought, because if a line of poetry strays into my memory, my skin bristles so that the razor ceases to act. This particular symptom is accompanied by a shiver down my spine; there is another which consists of a constriction of the throat and a precipitation of water to the eyes, and there is a third which I can only describe by borrowing a phrase from one of Keats' last letters, where he says, speaking of Fanny Brawne, 'everything that reminds me of her goes through me like a spear.' The seat of this sensation is the pit of the stomach."

you call it—being stricken and bitten by the words of his philosophy, which hold on more cruelly than the adder in the
soul of a young and not ungifted person, wherever they have
grasped it, and make him do and say whatever they will! I
see here Phaedrus, Agathon, Eryximachus, Pausanias, Aristodemus, Aristophanes—there is no need to mention Socrates
himself—and others of the same sort. All of you have had a
share of the madness and ecstasy of philosophy. (μανίας τε καὶ
βακχείας 217E–218B)

The bite of the snake is an image which carries forward the
metaphor of impregnation, but with emphasis upon the danger and
shock to mortals when they encounter the divine (a theme that is
ubiquitous in Greek myth). The Symposium emphasizes human
experiences as conventionally understood and interpreted. It might
seem from a first reading that Plato accepted as literal truth the
stories and myths of the Olympian pantheon. Yet the reinterpreta-
tion which Plato gives to Eros should warn us against such a facile
interpretation (as should remarks in the Euthyphro [6B], Phaedrus
[229cff] and Republic [377Dff]). By reinterpreting and clarifying
traditional religious enthusiasm Plato is able to achieve great relevance and inclusiveness for his theory of love—the passion of the
philosopher and scientist and poet—their sense that human life is
related to eternal values—is argued to have the same root as the
thrilling processions to Eleusis, and the frantic revels of the Corybantes.[10] Dramatically this connection between the highest and
most sophisticated human activities, and the most ordinary human
passions, is indicated when Socrates is praised by the drunken Alcibiades. Here the judgment of the most intense and sober reflection—represented in Socrates' speech—intermingles with the in-
stincts of a soul opened by wine, to the same effect: the greatest
love is the love of truth.

10. For an excellent discussion of this point, and Plato's general treatment of traditional religion, see John P. Anton's "Some Dionysian
References in the Platonic Dialogues," The Classical Journal, LVIII
(1962), 49–55.

The satyric image expresses perfectly what it is in Socrates' character that so fascinates Alcibiades: the paradoxical *combination* or *unity* of the "divine" and the "mortal." In Socrates great passion serves the most perfect unity of purpose; in him passion and strength of character and intellectual power are together in a harmony. To Alcibiades this combination of elements is an enigma, a juxtaposition of contrary ingredients. He can only grasp Socrates' nature through an image (which, revealing as it is, fails to relate the two factors functionally); beyond this his tongue cannot go. He tells the truth about Socrates, but cannot explain the inner springs, the motives and purposes, which make possible the portrait he presents. This bewildered admiration is closely linked with his dilemma as a person; he too contains "divine" and "mortal" elements, yet in violent and incurable opposition. It is thus most significant that his praise of Socrates should have the form of a history of their relationship; for his knowledge of Socrates is bound up with an awareness of this dilemma in himself.

Alcibiades' speech breaks down into three main parts. In the first part he speaks of the great emotional effect which Socrates' discourses always have on himself and others (215A–216C). In the second (216C–219D) he tells of attempting to win Socrates, to barter beauty for brains, after he had "looked inside the man" and seen those "divine and golden images." He is led here to a situation in which he is lover, Socrates beloved, but to no avail; this part closes with his "dishonor" and "humiliation." Thus his dilemma: Socrates has awakened his desires, he feels now a great need for knowledge and virtue—he has seen the beauty in them—yet to have what he desires he must give up illusions about himself and "tend to the wants of his own soul"; he can obtain virtue only at the expense of disvaluing his very remarkable personal endowments. But such a price is too high. He runs away from Socrates and gives in to popular acclaim, to which he is all beauty and power and goodness. As Agathon has also just begun to learn, the judgment of the wise and the many may conflict; and it is the latter Alcibiades has chosen to please. He thus relates—even with a certain surprise—that Socrates is the only person before whom he is ashamed (216B). At this point, where a stage of reflection might begin, Alcibiades' development and his relationship with Socrates stop because he refuses to turn inward. (The final one-third of his speech continues in its praise of Socrates, but Alcibiades is only a passive observer of him.) He notes his predicament; he has seen that there are greater things than wealth, bodily enjoyment, and medals of valor, because he knows a man who could have them and yet despises them; he has seen that there are greater beauties than his, greater songs than the tunes of Marsyus, greater soldiers than Laches, greater speakers than Pericles—and he is full of desire for greatness. Yet since the good things of life have been "proper" to him, given to him in homage to his greater goodness, he will accept a higher good only on condition that, like money or honor, it be placed at his feet. To sit until old age at the feet of Socrates is to him a preposterous yet unshakeable thought.

Alcibiades epitomizes in its extreme form what Plato believes to be the greatest danger to man—what we might with appropriate qualifications call excessive love of self. His pique is due to Socrates' unwillingness to give himself to him; he feels betrayed because Socrates, interested in his potentialities for good, appeared to be his lover yet was actually indifferent to those values which he and others loved in himself (his speech undoubtedly is, in part, a warning to Agathon that Socrates is no ordinary lover). To Plato the self is in large part a *power;* a power which manifests itself by giving form, order, beauty—not to the world, which is the province of god's activity—but to itself and the world of man. Being a power it reveals itself primarily in activity rather than repose, creativity rather than consumption. Yet its powers, to Plato, are dominated by a concern with value ("it shrivels up and withdraws in the presence of ugliness"), the love of good. Thus the self is concerned, aspires, loves, and toils on behalf of its love; it is bound up with an object of desire to which it relates itself in ever more or it may be ever less satisfying ways. The danger of Agathon and the failure of Alcibiades is to confuse the goal to which the self relates itself with *itself.* This confusion is the cause of Alcibiades' torment. For he feels at once that he is what he desires, that beauty and goodness are contained in himself, and that he must appropriate values which lie *outside*—power, wealth, glory, the wisdom of Socrates—fearing that without these he is nothing.

The *Symposium* does not contain a theory of the self, although it outlines with considerable care the dimensions of concern which preoccupy human beings. Its achievement is a rich and unitary image of human striving. The basis of the picture is the distinction between a world of becoming and being; its unity lies in the dominance of a principle of absolute value, beauty or good, over all aspects of human life. This picture contains the seeds of comedy and tragedy and the possibility of transcendence because the struggle is one which takes place within man himself. The domain of love is the domain of human concern, and love's character, great need and great cunning, is the character of man. Socrates as drawn in the *Symposium* is, like Eros, a messenger passing from the divine to the mortal. From his bantering with Aristodemus about who should go to whom—the good to the less good, the less good to the good—he becomes separate and abstract from the human world—in short an embodiment of the divine—on a porch near Agathon's house; then, having joined the bustle of the party bearing knowledge he cannot pour, like wine, into Agathon, he gradually ascends again, drawing his friends with him until they fall back into drunken exhaustion.

In the final scene Aristodemus observes Socrates, Aristophanes, and Agathon passing a large wine cup back and forth while Socrates argues that the arts of tragedy and comedy are essentially the same. Before the argument is completed however the two playwrights fall asleep, and Socrates leaves in the dawn to wash at the Lyceum. What is the significance of this scene? We should not invoke Aristotelian notions of tragedy to understand it, and in any case its meaning can be derived from the *Symposium* itself. Tragedy and comedy are, for Plato, two perspectives from which the human cycle of birth, struggle, and death may be viewed. The essentially comic arises whenever it is assumed that an absolute value has been realized in experience; comedy is the ridicule of this pretension. Tragedy likewise portrays the failure of man to achieve his highest goals, but mourns the inevitability of the loss. They are one because both are concerned with the same struggle and because both insist upon its ultimate failure.[11]

Socrates leaves the tragedian and comedian to their numan sleep. His departure is like a step upward beyond the realm of death and rebirth, into the clear light of eternity.*

J A B

11. My extrapolation of a Platonic theory of comedy and tragedy is admittedly speculative, nor can I do more here than indicate the sources on which a detailed justification would rely. I base my claims primarily on the role of Aristophanes in the *Symposium*, the remarks in this final scene taken in the context of the dramatic statement of the *Symposium* as a whole, and the treatment of comedy and tragedy in the *Republic* and the *Laws*.

* An earlier version of this essay was published in *Masterpieces of Western Literature: Contemporary Essays in Interpretation*, Alex Page and Leon Barron, eds. (Dubuque, Iowa: William C. Brown Co., Inc., 1966), vol. I, pp. 106–134. I am grateful to the editors and the publisher for permission to reprint.

Translator's Preface

The *Symposium* is one of the most beautiful and significant works of Western literature. It has a particularly poignant relevance to life in the late twentieth century and has been found exceptionally useful as an introductory text in numerous educational contexts. For these reasons there are currently in print more than seven English translations, reflecting among other things the nineteenth and twentieth centuries' changing attitudes toward Plato, toward love's role in society, and toward the purposes and responsibilities of translation itself.

The conditions under which translations are produced and used vary widely, but it is the nearly inevitable fate of any translation to evoke from the teacher of a text numerous strong and justified criticisms. These may be based on the fact that the translator has been concerned with the linguistic and aesthetic aspects of his rendering, or with achieving a literal adherence to the original, at the expense of the underlying ideas and philosophical ramifications which are the concerns of the class using the translation. As a result much class time may be devoted to correcting inaccuracies and confusions, particularly in translations of philosophers. On the other hand, translators whose main concern is the exact communication of ideas are often satisfied with pedantic, awkward, outdated English.

It was in the hope of producing a translation of the *Symposium* which reflected the considerations of a philosopher and poet, both devoted to Platonic thought and theory and the many charms of the dialogue, that this new version was undertaken. It is usually literal because a verbatim adherence to the dictionary meaning usually results in a clear and proper representation of the philosophical concepts as well as the literary form. But there are some places in the text where the translation becomes freer, where greater philosophical integrity seemed to the editor and translator to be achievable by a departure from such literalness. In such situations consistency has been sacrificed in favor of gaining for the reader a more precise and intelligible rendering of the Platonic idea.

There are, of course, a few instances where the Greek word simply will not submit itself to an English rendering, and here the reader has been advised of the difficulty by a footnote which explains the problem in some detail.

The 1909 Cambridge University Press edition of R. G. Bury's text with notes has been followed throughout.

S Q G

THE SYMPOSIUM OF PLATO

172 I believe I'm not unrehearsed in what you're asking. It happened recently that when I was coming to town from my home in Phalerum, one of my friends, sighting me ahead, called from far away, and having his joke at the same time, said:

Baldy Phalerian! You, Apollodorus! Won't you wait?

So I stopped and waited, and he said:

Apollodorus, I was looking for you just now. I wanted to
B ask you about that gathering at Agathon's. Those speeches about Love by Socrates and Alcibiades and the others who were there at the dinner, what were they like? Someone else told me what Phoenix, the son of Phillip told him, and he said that you know. He didn't tell it very clearly, though, so I wish you would tell me. It would be quite proper for you to recount the words of your friend. To begin with, he continued, tell me, were you or weren't you there in person at that gathering?
C Obviously your narrator wasn't very clear at all, I replied, if you imagine that the party where they talked about Love took place recently, and that I was there.

Oh, I did, he said.

How could I have been, Glaucon? Don't you realize that it is many years now since Agathon moved away from here, and that it is not three years since I became a companion of Socrates, and made it my business to know everything he says

173 and does every day? Before that I was running in circles, acting at random, thinking I was accomplishing something though I was unhappier than anyone, no less than you are now, imagining that anything was more necessary than philosophy.

Stop jeering, he said, just tell me when the party took place.

When we were still children, I said, and Agathon had won the prize with his first tragedy. It was the day after his victory celebrations with his cast.

It does sound like ancient history, he remarked, but who told you? Socrates himself?

B Heavens no, I replied, the same fellow who told Phoenix, a certain Aristodemus it was, from Cydathenaeum, the little fellow who's always barefoot—he was there at the party. I think he was one of Socrates' greatest admirers in those days. But then, too, I've asked Socrates himself about the things I heard from that fellow, and his account agrees exactly with what the man said.

Why, then, he asked, don't you tell me? The road we are taking to the city is just right for conversation.

So, you see, we went along, and as we walked we talked
C about this matter, and that's how it happens, as I said when we began, that I'm not unprepared, and if that's what you need to talk about, we must do so. As far as I'm concerned, any sort of philosophical discussion I have or listen to is immensely enjoyable, apart from its practical benefit. It's when I hear other kinds of talk, particularly the sort you have with the rich and with businessmen that I get angry, and pity you and your friends for thinking that you're accom-
D plishing something when, in fact, you're not doing a thing! I suppose, in turn, you think I'm unhappy, and I suppose you're right; but for my part it's not that I *think* it of you, I know it for a certainty!

Always the same, Apollodorus. You're always attacking yourself and others. It seems to me that you consider all men

utterly wretched, except for Socrates, beginning with yourself. Where you got your nickname 'maniac' I don't know,
but you always talk like one—raging against yourself and
others—everyone except Socrates!

E   Oh, my friend, is it so obviously madness and frenzy to
think this way about myself, and about you all?

There's no point to our wrangling about this business any
more, Apollodorus. Please, why don't you tell me about those
speeches, as I asked you?

The very same men who then—no—I would rather try to
174 tell it to you from the beginning, the way that fellow told me.

Socrates & Aristodemus

He says that he met Socrates coming from the baths, and that
he was wearing sandals, a thing the man rarely did. So he
asked him where he might be going, so handsomely got up.

To a dinner at Agathon's. I avoided him and the celebration
rites yesterday, for fear of the crowd, but I agreed to be
present today. I got dressed up like this so that beauty might
match beauty. But what about you, he went on, how about
B   it? Would you go to this dinner uninvited?

Oh, he said that he answered, I'll do just as you say.

Then follow, he urged, so that we can corrupt the saying
by turning it around, making it go: *To the feasts of a good
man the good go uninvited.* On his part, Homer not only
dares to corrupt the proverb, he outrages it! He sets Agamemnon up as an outstandingly good man in warfare, with
C   Menelaus the soft warrior. When Agamemnon has made a
sacrifice, he makes Menelaus go to the feast uninvited, the
lesser to the better.

I listened to this, he said, and answered, I'm afraid that it
isn't the way you represent it, Socrates, but Homer's way.
The one who is worthless—me—is going to the feast of the

wise man, unasked. So be ready to apologize for me, since I
D wouldn't agree to go without an invitation, unless you were
asking me.

When two, he quoted, *go together, one is ahead of the
other* in planning what we'll say. But let's get going.

The two of them went on talking in that sort of vein as
they walked along. But then Socrates drew his thoughts into
himself, and he was left behind to make his own way along
the road, having ordered the waiting Aristodemus to go on
E ahead. And when Aristodemus got to Agathon's house, he
discovered the door was open, and he said he felt rather foolish. A servant from inside met him immediately and led him
to where all the others were reclining and about to dine. Just
as soon as Agathon saw him, he said, he exclaimed:

Ah, I say, Aristodemus! It's a good thing, your coming
just now to eat with us! Now, if you've come for any other
reason, why put it off for another time. I looked for you
yesterday in order to invite you, but I didn't find you! But
how is it you haven't brought Socrates to us?

And I turned around, he said, but could see nothing of
Socrates behind me. I said then that I had actually come with
Socrates, since he had invited me there to dinner.

And right you were to do so, he said, but where is he?

175 He was right behind me just a minute ago—but now I'm
wondering, myself, where he can be.

Why don't you see if you can find Socrates? Agathon said
to a servant, and bring him to us. And you, Aristodemus, sit
down beside Eryximachus.

And so he tells that a servant helped him wash up, so that he
might recline at the table, and that another of the servants
came with the report that Socrates himself, who had stopped
at a neighbor's, was standing outside on his porch; when
he was asked to come in, he didn't wish to do so.

How strange, Agathon said. But go on calling him, and
don't give up.

B No, by all means leave him alone! He has a way of doing
this. Sometimes he goes into a trance just where he happens

to be standing. He'll come back presently, I know it. Don't move him—let him be!

Well then that's how it'll have to be if you feel that way, he has Agathon say. So, servants, attend to the others. Set things out exactly as you'd like, seeing as no one is directing you (I've never done this before). Make believe that I've been invited to dinner by you, and these other people too. Take care of us, so that we can congratulate you.

C   After this business, he says, they started to eat without Socrates. Agathon kept ordering someone to go get Socrates, but Aristodemus wouldn't allow it. He didn't linger as long as he usually did, so that when he did arrive they were at most half-way through dinner. Thereupon Agathon—since he happened to be situated at the end, alone—is said to have called:

D   Here, Socrates, sit by me and eat so by touching you I may partake of some of that wisdom which has come to you on the porch. Clearly you found what you were searching after and have it, or you wouldn't have left there.

And Socrates sat down, remarking: I wish, Agathon, that wisdom were the sort of thing that could flow from the fuller of us to the emptier by our touching one another, the way, for instance, in the case of cups, water flows through wool from the fuller to the emptier. If wisdom were like that I'd

E   value this seat beside you very much. I know I'd be filled with a great deal of very beautiful wisdom from you. My own is paltry and ambiguous, it has the nature of a dream, while yours glistens and is so full and generous. It radiated brilliantly from your youth and came to light just the other day, for a witness of more than thirty thousand Greeks!

You're mocking me, Socrates, Agathon protested. You and I can carry on our arguments about wisdom a little later, and have Dionysus as judge. But for now just apply yourself to dinner.

176   After this, he relates, Socrates settled down and ate with the others. Their libations were made, the proper devotions were paid to the god, and the other things that are required

were done. They turned to the drinking. Then, he tells me, Pausanias began with a speech that went something like this:

Well then, gentlemen, how shall we go about this drinking with the greatest ease? I, for one, announce that I am in a thoroughly wretched state, thanks to yesterday's drinks, and I could use some respite. My guess is you're all in the same condition; you were there yesterday, yourselves. So let's try to find some way to drink without discomfort.

B

Then Aristophanes declared, It's quite true, what you say, Pausanias. We must find some way of drinking that'll be easy on us. I got pretty well soaked yesterday, too!

Hearing their remarks, Eryximachus, Acoumenus' son, said, What you're saying is quite true, but there's something else to be asked. How does Agathon feel about a resolution to drink?

Not at all, he said, I'm not up to it.

C

It would be a godsend for us, it seems, he said, for me and Aristodemus and Phaedrus and these fellows, if you strongest ones put a stop to your drinking. We're always the feeble ones. (I leave Socrates out of it, he's fine either way—he'll be satisfied with whichever we do). Then since it seems to me that no one here is eager for any heavy wine-drinking, I will probably be less likely to cause displeasure by speaking the truth about the nature of intoxication. I think that it becomes

D

obvious when one is a doctor, what an evil inebriation is for mankind. I myself don't voluntarily drink beyond a certain limit, and would counsel another person not to either, particularly when he is still hungover from the preceding day.

Well then, here he reports that Phaedrus the Myrrhinousian spoke.

I myself am usually persuaded by you, particularly in medical matters, but in this matter the others, too, would do well to take your counsel.

E

At this they all agreed not to turn the get-together into an occasion for drunkenness, and to drink only so far as it gave pleasure.

And what's more, went on Eryximachus, now that we've decreed that each man should drink as he wants, and not under compulsion, I propose our bidding farewell to that flute-girl who just came in. She can play for herself, or, if she wants, for the women inside, and leave us to talk with one another today. And I'd like to suggest a topic for discussion, if you agree.

177 Well, they did all agree, and urged him to make his proposal. And Eryximachus went on.

I will begin my words after the manner of Euripides' Melanippe: *as what I will say isn't my own*—but Phaedrus'. Phaedrus is always complaining to me like this: Isn't it a shame, Eryximachus, he says, that the poets compose hymns and paeans to all the other gods, but to Love, who is so great and venerable a god, not a single poem or song of praise has ever been composed by anyone of all the poets who have ever lived? And then, too, when you review the good philosophers, who write dissertations praising, say, Heracles and others, the way the eminent Prodicus does—this in itself is not so surprising, but I've actually come upon a book in which salt was given fantastic praise for its usefulness, and you could find a lot of other things of the same ilk receiving eulogies. Now while they make up such things with all that enthusiasm, no man to this day has ever tried to sing the praises of Love as befits him! No, they neglect so great a god! To my mind Phaedrus is quite right, and accordingly I'll willingly give in to him and make my contribution, but, in addition, I see this occasion as a fitting one, with us gathered here, to celebrate the god. So then, if you agree too, it might be pleasant for us to spend the time discoursing. I think the best way would be for each of us to make a speech in praise of Love, going around to the right, and to do so as beautifully as possible. Phaedrus should start first, both because he is sitting in the first position, and because he is, as it were, the father of the idea!

No one will vote you down, Eryximachus, remarked Soc-

44

E rates. I certainly could never refuse, since I claim I understand nothing but love-matters, nor should Agathon and Pausanias, nor Aristophanes, who devotes himself entirely to Dionysus and Aphrodite, nor any other of the people I see here. Of course, it's unfair to those of us who are sitting at the end; but if those who come first speak properly and beautifully, we'll be satisfied. But let Phaedrus get started, and good luck to him! Let's have his praise of Love!

178 To this all the others gave their assent, and commanded Phaedrus to begin. Everyone of them spoke on this subject, but Aristodemus didn't remember every detail, and now I've even forgotten some of what he told me. But I'll tell you what I think to be most memorable from each one's speech.

Phaedrus

First of all then, as I've said, he describes Phaedrus as starting roughly like this—saying that Love was truly a great god, marvelous to men and gods alike in a lot of different ways,
B and not the least of these was the matter of his birth:

He is honored as the most ancient among the gods, and here is the proof of it: No one knows or tells anything about the birth of Love, in either prose or poetry. Hesiod does say that in the beginning there was chaos,

> but then, full-breasted Earth, the eternal safe resting place of all things, and Love.

Both Hesiod and Acusilaus agree that after chaos, Earth and Love came together into being. And Parmenides says of the Beginning:

> First of all was Love, out of all the gods, created.

C So, there is agreement on many sides that Love is the oldest of them all. And as he is the oldest he is the source of the greatest blessings to us. I can't describe any greater blessing

to a person in his earliest youth, than a good lover, and to a
lover, his young friend. What men must follow for their
entire lives if they intend to live beautifully and well, neither
D   family nor public honors, nor wealth, nor anything else, can
implant so well as Love.

So I ask, what is this thing? It is the feeling of shame, on
the one hand, before shameful deeds, and the desire, on the
other, to emulate noble ones. And without these neither a
state nor an individual can achieve anything great and noble.

What is more, I say that if one loves a person, and happens
to be exposed in a vile act or in cowardly submission to something vile, one would suffer less from being seen by his
father or his comrades, or by any other, than by his young
E   friend. In exactly the same way we see how extremely
ashamed the beloved is before his lovers if he is observed in
some shameful act.

See then, if some device could be invented whereby a state
or army could be made into a colony of lovers and their
youths, it would be impossible to lead a better life than with
179   these same people shunning all disgrace and striving to earn
one another's respect. When they fought others, these lovers
would win over all, though they were few, as the saying goes.
A man in love would far less willingly be seen deserting his
post or surrendering his arms by his young friend than by all
the others, and would sooner embrace death. Then, to leave
the youth behind, or to fail to rescue him when he was in
danger—no one is so low that Love couldn't inspire him with
such valor that he would become equal to the greatest of
B   spirits! And frankly, when Homer says that a god *breathed
a wrath* into certain of the heroes, he is talking about what
Love instills in lovers.

Further, only lovers desire to die for their beloveds, and
this is not only true of men, but women as well. Here Pelius'
daughter Alcestis provides ample testimony to Greeks in
support of my claim, because only she was willing to die in
C   her husband's place, though he had a father and mother. Be-

cause she loved, she surpassed them in affection, so much that she rendered these people strangers to their son, relatives in name only. When she had gone through with it her deed seemed so beautiful, not only to men but to the gods, that they granted her the gift which very few of the many who have performed numerous noble acts are given: they brought her soul back from Hades—they admired her deed so.

D   So, even the gods give great honor to earnestness and courage in love. But then again, they sent Orpheus, the son of Oeagrus, away out of Hades without success. They allowed him the shade of the woman for whom he had come but did not give *her* up, because he showed himself weak—he played the cithera—and lacking in the courage to die for his love, the way Alcestis had done, for he contrived to get down to Hades while still alive. It was on account of this that they

E   made him suffer the penalty of death at the hands of women. But they honored Achilles, the son of Thetis, whom they sent to the Islands of the Blessed because, after learning from his mother that he would himself die once he had killed Hector, and that if he didn't kill him he could go home and live to be an old man, he dared to choose to help his lover

180 Patroclus, and having avenged him, not only to die for his sake, but to join in death the friend whose life had ended. The gods were exceedingly pleased by this, and honored him especially, because he had made so much of his friend. Oh, Aeschylus mixes it all up and says that it was Achilles who pursued Patroclus—Achilles!—who was more glorious, not only than Patroclus, but than all of the heroes put together, and still without a beard, because, as Homer says, he was the

B   younger! But, in reality, the gods honor most the virtue that comes in love; they would treasure, would delight in, would benefit a person if, being wooed, he loved his lover, more than if he pursued a youth as a lover! A lover is more divine than the youth he loves. He is inspired. Because of this they honored Achilles more than Alcestis, and sent him to the Islands of the Blessed.

So, you see, I assert that of the gods Love is the most ancient, the most honorable and the most benevolent in bestowing virtue and happiness on men, alive and dead.

C He reports that Phaedrus gave his speech like that, and after Phaedrus came some others whose speeches he couldn't completely remember. So he skipped over them and came to Pausanias' oration. It began:

Pausanias

It seems to me, Phaedrus, that this arrangement won't work out well for us, if we are simply supposed to invent talks in praise of Love. It'd be fine if Love were one thing; but it isn't one. And in view of its not being one it would be better,

D first, to say which form of Love we're supposed to praise. I'm going to try, then, to set this business straight, beginning with a discussion of the specific Love one ought to praise, and then praising the god appropriately.

We all know that Aphrodite is never without Love. And if she were one there would be a single Love. But since there are actually two Aphrodites, it is necessary to assume two Loves as well. And can anyone challenge the notion of the bifold goddess? On one side we have the ancient one, the motherless daughter of Uranos, whom we even call 'Uranian,' or 'celestial.' Then there is the younger one, the child of Zeus and Dione, whom we address as 'Pandemus'—or 'common.'

E It is necessary to describe Love, too, as 'common' when he is engaged with the younger Aphrodite and as 'celestial' when with the former. One ought to praise all gods, but I'll try to describe the attributes of each of these two separately.

181 Every action has this about it: of itself its performance is neither good nor bad. It's this way for our behavior now—if we drink or sing or converse—none of these acts is particularly noble, but rather it's how the deed is done that makes

the difference. If it is done in a noble manner and properly it becomes noble, and if improperly, ignoble. Thus I say that even loving and Love are not wholly good, nor worthy of praise, but only that loving which urges us toward noble action.

B   Now the Love of the common Aphrodite is truly common, and works at random; it is this one your average man loves. First of all, such men love women no less than boys; then, whomever they love, it is their bodies rather than their souls; then, it is the shallowest people they can find, wanting only to have them, without any concern for the beauty of the thing or its lack. These people take it as it happens to come, and go to, good or bad. This is the nature of the god who

C comes from that younger goddess, whose birth partook of a mixture of female and male.

Then there is the Love of the celestial goddess, who does not partake of the female, only of the male; then, she is older and entirely lacks lust. Men who have been inspired by this Love turn to the male, loving what is most vigorous and more intelligent. And anyone would know, even in this matter of love for young boys, those who are purely involved in this

D love; they don't desire boys until they are beginning to think, just about the same time that the beard is starting to grow. I believe that people who begin at that point to fall in love, are prepared to share their lives completely, even to live together. They are not deceivers who thoughtlessly will take such a boy, and then laugh and turn away to live with another.

But there must be a law against one's loving young boys,

E so that a great deal of zeal won't be wasted on an uncertainty. It is uncertain what the boys will grow up to be, what evil or good they will end up having in body and soul. And while good men lay down this law for themselves and hold themselves to it, it is necessary to force the vulgar sort of lovers to

182 adhere to it, just the way we force them, as far as we are able, not to make love to our free women. It is this kind who

have introduced the disgrace that makes some men go so far as to say that it is low to gratify lovers—but they say this when they regard the sort I'm describing, observing their importunity and unfairness. If the deed were performed decently and it had a sure legality, they could not justly hold it in reproach.

In other cities the law that deals with love-making is easy to understand, it is simply defined. But the one we have here
B   is complicated. Take Elis, for example, and Boeotia, and places where they are not so articulate. It is set down plainly in the law that to give oneself to lovers is a good thing, nor would anyone, young or old, say it was bad. They wouldn't want, I believe, to have to do the job of convincing the boys of it, and pleading an argument, as they are unskilled in speaking. However, in Ionia, and in many other places it is decreed a bad thing, to the extent that they live under bar-
C   barians. Since the barbarians live under tyrants this is made a disgrace, as are philosophy and athletics. It isn't expedient, I imagine, for the rulers, if any deep thoughts develop in their subjects, nor strong friendships and comradeships, and actually, all the very things Love delights in engendering. The tyrants have learned this fact from the experience here. The love of Aristogeiton and the affection of Harmodius, when it had grown constant, destroyed their power. So, where it has been held an evil to give oneself to lovers, it is because
D   of the evil of those who made the laws. On the one hand it stems from the arrogance of the rulers, and on the other from the emasculated cowardice of the ruled. However, if it has been ruled by law to be entirely good, this is the case because of an intellectual laziness in the lawmakers. Here, the law that deals with these matters is far better, but as I said before, it's not easy to understand.

Consider that it is said to be better to love openly than secretly, and especially finest to love the highest in mind and the noblest, even when they are uglier than others. Further-
E   more, one is cheered on marvelously in this love by every-

body: one never does anything disgraceful; being won seems
a fine thing, and it seems base not to be; and the law grants
freedom to a lover who is trying to catch his beloved by
doing marvelous deeds to win him praise, while the very
183 same acts, if done by someone pursuing and wanting some
other end, would bring the greatest reproach.

If one wanted to get wealth from someone, or to attain an
office or some other power, and wanted to use the same
methods that lovers use with their youths (making supplica-
tions and entreaties in prayers, and swearing oaths and sleeping at their doorsteps, and desiring to perform menial tasks
such that no slave would be willing to perform), he would be
B   prevented from acting out this business by his friends and
by his enemies alike. The latter would reproach him for his
obsequiousness and slavishness, while the former would chastise him and be ashamed over these things. But in a lover
who does all these things one sees some grace. He is allowed
by law to act without reproach, as if he were performing
acts that were thoroughly noble. But what is strangest of all is
how the people say that the gods will give pardon to him
alone when he swears on oath and then breaks it; for an oath
of someone under Aphrodite's rule, they say, doesn't exist—
C   so that both men and gods give complete freedom to the
lover, as the law says here.

For this reason a person might well think that it is ruled
completely honorable here in this city, both to be a lover,
and to be affectionate to lovers. But fathers have appointed
tutors for those who are being wooed, so that they won't be
allowed to hold intercourse with their lovers, and restrictions
are imposed by the tutor to this end, and the boy's comrades
D   and friends reproach him whenever they see this sort of thing
taking place, nor do the elders check the reproachers, nor
abuse them as speaking out of turn, so that when one has
observed such things one would believe rather that this sort
of thing is considered execrable here. But I think that this
is how it really is: it isn't simple, as I said at the outset, but the

granting of one's affection is, of itself, neither a noble thing, nor deplorable. It is a beautiful act if done beautifully, and if lowly, low. It is done basely when one gives one's affections to a base person, and does so in a low manner; when one does so to a good man, and in a noble way, it is done beautifully. The man who is a lover in the common way is
E base—he loves the body rather than the soul. Nor is he constant, since he loves things which lack constancy. Why, with the flower of the body fading, his favor, too, *disappearing, is gone*—and his many speeches and promises are discredited. But the person who loves the character of a good man en-
184 dures throughout life, merging with what is lasting.

Now, our law attempts to prove men in a good and accurate way, those to whom one should yield, and those one ought to avoid. By these means it encourages us to pursue some people and flee from others, acting as referee, and making judgments about lover and beloved. That's why it's customarily considered an ignominy to be won quickly. It's so that time might pass, since time does seem to prove most things well. Then, too, it's held a lowness to grant
B favors on account of wealth and political power, in case one were suffering miserably from fear, lacked endurance, was unable to scorn the benefits of property or political success, or else were yielding in the hope of receiving some benefit. These things seem to lack steadiness and constancy. Besides, genuine friendship will not arise from this kind of relationship. One path, then, is left us by our legal institution, if
C the darling is to gratify his lover honorably. Just as it is not considered flattery or anything to be ashamed of when lovers want to serve and act like slaves for their beloved youths, so in the same way our law allows one other form of voluntary servility to be kept without shame; and this is when it is done for the sake of virtue.

It is our wont not to consider his willing slavery execrable, or anything to be ashamed of, when a man desires to serve someone and is led by this person to become better, either in

wisdom or some other part of virtue. One must combine
D   both conventions—the one concerning pederasty, and this
one, which deals with philosophy and other virtues—then one
may conclude that it is a good thing for a young boy to
yield to an admirer. When the lover and his darling come to
one another, and each holds to his own law: the one justly
doing any sort of service whatever for his sweetheart, and
the other justly complying, in all ways, with the man who is
making him wise and good; the former being capable of
E   endowing intellectuality and other virtues, and the latter
needing to acquire knowledge; when these principles have
coincided at the same point, then and only then is there a
nobility in the beloved youth's acquiescing to his lover. In
other circumstances, there is none. Furthermore, in this situation, there is no disgrace for a person who is betrayed,
whereas in all others, whether one is betrayed or not, the
185   relationship carries with it disgrace. If someone yields to a
lover for his wealth and is deceived and receives no money
because the lover turns out to be poor, it is still disgraceful.
He shows himself to be the sort who will do anything for
anyone, if money will result. There is no honor in this. But
then, by the same token, if one gives oneself in love to a man
whom one supposes to be good, for the sake of growing to
B   be a better person through one's friend's affection, and then is
deceived because the man turns out to be evil and lacking
in virtue, the deception is just as honorable. One has in all
this proven oneself, in that one could utterly adore someone
for the sake of becoming a person of deeper virtue. This is
a thing of the greatest beauty, and for this reason I feel that to
give oneself for the sake of virtue is thoroughly noble. Such
love is the love of the heavenly goddess, celestial, and precious to many, both publicly and privately, compelling a
C   lover and the one beloved to show great concern for their
virtue. All the other sorts of love are of the other goddess, the
earthly one.

And this, he concluded, is my contribution to you, on

Love, Phaedrus, and I have just thrown it together!

When Pausanias had *paus*ed (heh, heh—get it? my professors taught me how to pun like this)—Aristodemus said it was Aristophanes' turn to speak, but it happened that, either because of his eating too much, or for some other reason, he had a fit of hiccupping and was unable to deliver his

D speech, but said—since Eryximachus the doctor was placed just below him in order:

Eryximachus, be a good fellow and cure my hiccupping, or else speak for me, so that I can stop it.

And Eryximachus replied, Oh, but I'll do both those things. To start with I'll talk in your place, and when you've stopped hiccupping, you can talk in mine. But while I'm speaking, perhaps the hiccups will decide to leave if you hold

E your breath for a long time, and if they don't, gargle with water. If they are really stubborn, take something that is likely to tickle your nostrils, and sneeze! If you do this once or twice it'll go away, no matter how stubborn it is.

The sooner you speak the better, said Aristophanes, and I'll do what you say. So Eryximachus spoke.

Eryximachus

Well then, it appears to me to be necessary, since although

186 Pausanias spoke beautifully at the outset, his conclusion was insufficient, it is necessary, I say, for me to attempt to append a conclusion to his argument. To begin with, to say that Love is dichotomous seems to me perfectly valid; but it moves the hearts of men not only toward beautiful human beings but also toward many other things, and is in other things: is in the bodies of all things living, even things that grow in the earth, and, in a word, in everything that exists. This seems, from the medical point of view, to be true; and men in our

B field have seen how great and wonderful is this god who

vibrates in everything, human and divine. I shall begin by talking from this medical point of view because I respect the science so much.

It is the nature of the body to manifest Pausanias' two-fold Love. For health and disease in a body are admittedly different and distinct, and different things desire and love different things. Thus, while desire is one thing in a healthy body, it is another in one diseased. And just as Pausanias said before,

C it is a beautiful thing for one to yield in love to good men, but base to obscene ones. Then, too, in the body itself, it is fine and even proper to yield to the good and wholesome wants of every body, and this is what is called therapy, but it is bad to yield to the noxious and evil desires. They will be rejected by anyone proficient in the art. For this is what medicine is, to put it summarily, a knowledge of the forces of

D Love in the body, for being stuffed and emptied out; and a person who can accurately diagnose whether the noble or the vulgar love is functioning in these cases and can interchange them is a master therapist. Thus, by eliminating one love and replacing it with the other, and knowing when to implant love when it ought to be introduced, and when to extract improper desires when they are present, one may be said to be an able practitioner. For one must, as a matter of fact, make the most antagonistic elements in the body friendly and loving to one another. The most antagonistic things are direct opposites: cold to heat, bitter to sweet, dry

E to moist, and so on, in all such cases. Our forefather Asclepius, who established our profession, knew how to impart love and concord to these things, as these poets here have said and I believe it.

So that medicine, accordingly, is ruled throughout by this

187 god, and so likewise gymnastics and agriculture. In the case of music too, as is perfectly obvious to anyone who has given the slightest thought to these matters, it is just as Heracleitus tried to point out, although he didn't word it very well. For *The one*, he says, *a thing in discord with itself, is drawn into union, just as in the case of the harmony of bow and*

lyre. But it is utterly illogical to speak of a harmony in discord, or of its coming out of discordant things. Rather, he seems to be saying in this that by the art of music it is out of

B things that are discordant *at first*, as treble and bass, that later on a concord develops. But it isn't really out of the *discord* between treble and bass that harmony arises. Harmony is consonance, and consonance a kind of concord. For concord to arise from discord while the elements are discordant is an impossibility. But then again, a kind of variance that is not incapable of reconciliation can be harmonized, as, say,

C rhythm develops out of the swift and slow, at variance to begin with, but later reconciled. Just as earlier it was medicine, so here it is music that brings the concord to all these cases, implanting a mutual love and harmony; and so, music is a science of love, relating to harmony and rhythm. It is not difficult to recognize the love-forces in this actual establishment of harmony and rhythm, and here it is not the twofold Love that is at work.

But when it becomes necessary in the world of men to

D apply rhythm and harmony—or composition—what people call 'song writing,' or else when someone makes arrangements of the melodies and meters already composed—which is called 'pedagogy,' then difficulty arises, and there is need for a good craftsman. And here the earlier principle comes up again, that one ought to give oneself to decent men or to those who aren't but would be made more decent, and to cherish the love of these men, and that this is the noble, heav-

E enly Love, which is of the Muse Urania. On the other hand, that of Polymnia, the mundane kind, one ought to indulge being careful about those with whom one indulges, so that one may reap pleasure for oneself, without taking on any indecency. It is just as in my profession, where one has to exercise great effort to make proper use of the desire men have for good cooking, so that pleasure can be taken without sickness.

Indeed, in music and in medicine, and in all the other instances of human and divine activity as well, so far as is

188   possible one should take careful note of each of the loves. Each will be present.

Since even the arrangement of the seasons of the year is full with both of these Loves, and when the things which I was just talking about happen to occur together through the functioning of the orderly love-force—that is, the hot and the cold, the dry and the wet—they achieve a harmony and synthesis when they occur in due proportion, they appear as purveyors of a good harvest, of well-being to men and other animals and plants, and there is no injustice. But when Love, in pride, becomes too strong in the control of the seasons

B   of the year, there is much destruction and injustice. Plagues love to develop out of just these sorts of things, and many other lawless maladies among flora and fauna, such as hoar-frosts, hailstorms and mildews, arise out of a grasping excessiveness and disorder of these love-forces toward one another.

The knowledge of these love-forces, when it concerns the courses of the stars, and the seasons of the year is called 'astronomy.'

So too all the sacrifices and things over which the art of

C   divination has control—that is, the intercourse that gods and mortals have with one another—concern nothing other than the preservation and cure of Love. For every impiety loves to develop when someone has not gratified the orderly Love, or has, in every affair, honored and revered not him but the other, where one's parents are concerned (whether they're alive or dead), as well as where the gods are concerned. It has been assigned to divination to oversee these forces of

D   love, and treat them; and divination is the craft responsible for the affections that exist between men and gods. It knows the forces of love in men, and draws them toward what is decent and holy.

Thus Love in his totality holds much great, no, in brief, complete power, and the good he accomplishes with moderation and justice among us and among the gods, this is his greatest power, and through this provides us with a complete

joy. It is what makes us able to be with one another, and to
be the friends of those who are mightier than us, the gods.

Thus, whereas I may well have left out many of the things
that can be said in praise of Love, it was not on purpose, of
course; but if I have omitted something, it'll be your job,
Aristophanes, to complete the picture. However, if you plan
to make your encomium to this god in a completely different
way, begin your praise, since you've definitely gotten over
your hiccups.

Then he said that Aristophanes started to talk and began
with: Yes, it has stopped completely, but only after I applied
the sneeze treatment to it! I wonder if the regular principle
of my body lusts after such blasts and ticklings as there are in
sneezing—it honestly stopped completely when I used the
sneeze on it!

Aristophanes, m'love, exclaimed Eryximachus, look out for
what you say! You're clowning before you begin and forcing me to guard against any foolishness you may talk, when
you could speak in peace!

And Aristophanes, laughing, said, Oh you're right, Eryximachus; I unsay all I've said! But don't be so guarded against
me—as far as what I'm going to say is concerned, I'm not
so much worried that I'll produce a *farce* (*that'd* be a feather
in my cap, it's natural to my Muse)—I'm afraid of being
ridiculous!

Do you think you can just strike and run, Aristophanes?
Speak your piece but be ready to defend yourself. There is a
chance that I may be persuaded to let you off.

Aristophanes

But of course, Eryximachus, said Aristophanes, I'm planning
to make my talk rather different from yours and Pausanias'.
It seems to me that men don't understand the power of Love

at all—if they did, he would have the biggest temples and altars, and people would offer the greatest sacrifices to him. As things stand, nothing like this exists, and he's the greatest
D of them all! He is the god who loves men most. He helps them and cures them of those things whose cures provide the greatest joy for mankind. So I'll try to get you to realize the power of this god. Then you, in turn, can be the teachers for others.

To begin with, you must grasp the true nature of mankind and its sufferings. Our nature wasn't originally what it is now. No, it was quite different. First of all, there were three
E kinds of men, not two as now, the male and the female, but also a third kind combining both. We have the name still, but the thing itself has disappeared. The androgyne, separate in name and nature, partook of man and woman both. But the name is used now only as a reproach. Then also people were shaped like complete spheres. Their backs and sides made a circle. They had four hands, with the same number of legs
190 and two faces—completely the same—on top of a circular neck. These two faces were set on opposite sides of one head, with four ears. And there were two sets of sexual parts, and whatever else one imagines goes along with this arrangement.

They walked around quite upright, just as we do today, but in whichever direction they chose, and whenever they got running fast, it was just like acrobats revolving in a
B circle—legs straight out and somersaulting! But then they had eight limbs to use for support when they were rolling swiftly around in circles! The three sexes were like this: the male was descended, in the beginning, from the sun, and the female from the earth, and the one that partook of both of them came from the moon, because the moon itself partakes of the natures of those two. So these things were globes themselves, you know, and took after their ancestors in the way they got around. In fact, they had terrific power and energy, were arrogant, and assaulted the gods. The story in Homer about
C Ephialtes and Otus is told of these: how they were set on

while ascending to heaven to launch an attack against the gods.

Then Zeus and the other gods went into a huddle over what had to be done about these creatures, but they were baffled. They were not willing to destroy them and obliterate the race with a blast of lightning, like the giants, since their sacrifices and honors would be lost along with mankind. Nor would they swallow this wanton behavior. Finally, after a tremendous lot of pondering, Zeus said:

D   I think I have a scheme whereby men may exist yet stop their licentiousness: we'll debilitate them. We'll slice each of them into two, he said, and they shall both be weakened and more useful to us, through the increase in their numbers. And if their wantonness seems to continue and they refuse to buckle under, why, he went on, I'll slice them in two again! They can go around then on one foot, hoppity-hop!

Thus he spoke, and he cut each man in two, the way people cut sorb apples to make preserves (or the way they do eggs

E   with hairs). And for each one he cut, he set Apollo to turning the face and half of the neck around, towards the cut, so that in contemplating his incision a man might be made more orderly. Then he told him to heal them up.

So Apollo turned their heads around, and pulled the skin together from all sides to what is now called the stomach, like we do with round pouches with drawstrings. Leaving the one opening, he made a knot at the middle of the stomach,

191 what they call the navel. He rubbed smooth many other rough spots, and moulded the breast, using the sort of tool shoemakers use on their lasts when they smooth away the side wrinkles. He left a few, though, around the stomach and navel, to serve as a reminder of past sufferings.

Now since the natural form of man had been severed into two parts and each half yearned for its match, when they met, they would throw their arms about one another and get

B   enmeshed together. They yearned to grow together, and because they didn't want to do anything apart from one another, they began to die from hunger and inactivity. Whenever one of the halves died, and one was left, it would hunt around and get itself involved with another, either a hemi-woman—which we now simply call woman—or hemi-man, it might meet. But they were dying off this way, so Zeus, taking pity on them, devised another plan. He set their genitals around in the front (until this time they had had them behind, and they had fertilized and begat, not with one another, but on the ground like grasshoppers). So he set them around,

c this way, on the front, and that way got them to propagate with one another, with the male's inside the female. On account of this, if a man happened to come to a woman, while they were embracing she would conceive and they'd have a baby. If it happened between two men they'd simply have the pleasure of being together but then they'd stop, and turn to their labors, and pay some attention to the rest of life.

d So that's how it is, you see, that the love of one another is ingrained in men, ever since that time. It restores his ancient nature to man, and ventures to make one out of two, and heal the human condition.

Each of us, then, is the matching half of a man, because we were sliced like flatfish, and two were made out of one! And everybody carries on an eternal search for his other half. Those among men who are halves cut from the middle sex, the one that was called 'androgyne' in those days, are lovers

e of women. Lots of philanderers descend from this sort. Then, adultresses and women who are man-crazy come from this same sex. However, women who were sliced from the total woman have no predilection for men. They are strongly drawn to other women, and the "inverts" are derived from this sort. Those who have been cut from the whole male

192 befriend men, and lying with them, and performing acts of love, yield themselves to men. This sort make for the noblest of boys and young men. They have the most courageous natures. The people who speak of these fellows as shameless are wrong. They don't do it out of shamelessness, but courage.

It's done in virility and manliness, because they cherish what is like themselves. And here is further proof: the only men of this sort who succeed in public affairs are adults who were like that as boys. When they grow to manhood they take to boys, and it isn't by nature that they take any interest in marriage and family life, but are only pressured into it by convention. It would suffice for them to live with one another without marrying. This sort of man is born to pederasty and eroticism and always welcomes one like himself with open arms.

So that whenever the pederast, or any other sexual type, meets a half that is the same sort, they are overwhelmed with wonder by the affection, the joy of intimacy, and the love. They don't ever want, one might say, to be separated from one another, not even for a second. These people, living their entire lives together like this, wouldn't be able to articulate what it is they want to happen between them. Nor would anyone believe that such a union is only sexual, or that two people who share a mutual love have such a great passion for sex. But clearly there is something else that the soul of each desires, which it is unable to articulate, but it does divine and feel a hint of what it wants.

Imagine Hephaestus standing over them as they were lying together in this embrace, with his tools ready, and he says: 'What is it you want, you humans, to take place between you?' And suppose he addressed them again, as they lay helpless: 'So, do you want to be melded together as much as possible, and not have to leave one another, night or day? If this is what you want, I am willing to join you and weld you into one and the same being. You'll become one self out of two, and you can live as one, with the two of you sharing a life in common as a single being. And when you die, there in Hades, too, instead of two there will be one and you will share death. But look—is this what you want? Will you be satisfied if this should happen?' We know that not a single one of them would refuse such an offer. They would seem to

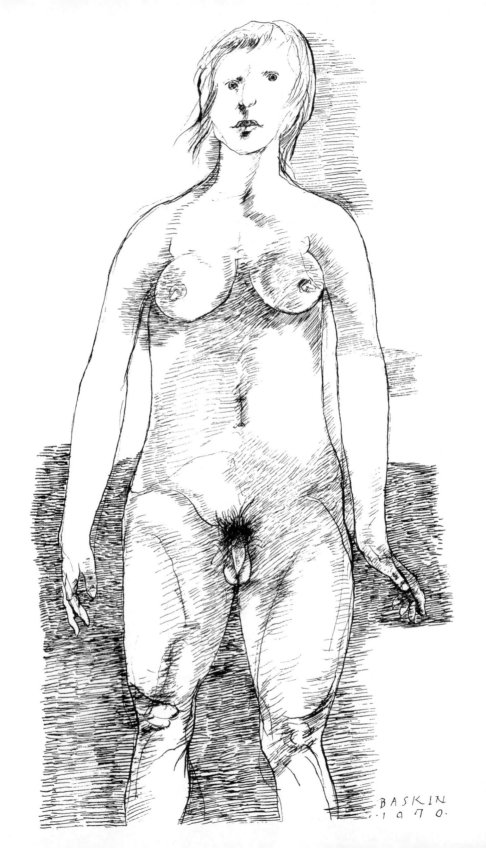

BASKIN
·1970·

desire nothing else. Everyone would openly acknowledge this as the age-old desire—the coming together and merging with the one they love so that the two become one.

The reason for this is that our original nature was to be whole. And to the longing for wholeness the name 'love' has been attached. In the old days, as I've said, we were one; but now, on account of our crime, we have been split up by god (just the way the Arcadians were by the Lacedaemonians). Then, too, there is a fear that if we don't carry on our relationship with the gods in the proper way we'll be cut in two again. Then we'd have to go around mere outlines, and like the bas-relief carvings on pillars, be sawn through the nostrils, like split dice. That's why it behooves everybody to be obedient and worshipful to the gods. That way we can escape these consequences, and have good luck with the power of Love as our leader and marshal. No one should do anything in opposition to him—the man who does act in opposition is hateful to the gods—*we* must be the friends of god. If we are on good terms with him we will find happiness and be able to get together with the very boys we should, which few of us can claim to have done as of now! But I hope Eryximachus won't refute me with ridicule, as if I were talking about Pausanias and Agathon! Oh, I suppose it's true that they have had the experiences I'm referring to, and both have male natures. But really, I'm talking about all men and women. Our race can become happy if we satisfy desire, and if each can find his proper darling and return to his original, natural state. If this is the best thing, then, by necessity, what in our present circumstances comes closest to it is best for now. That is to find a love who is of like mind to oneself. So, really, if we are going to sing the praises of the god who can realize this with all justice, we should sing for Love. He can help us the most at present by drawing each together with his own. And he gives us great hope, that if we offer proper worship to the gods, he can restore us to our original condition, and by his healing, make us happy and joyful!

This, Eryximachus, he said, is my speech on Love, quite different from yours. So, as I begged of you, don't ridicule it, so that we can hear all of the remaining speakers—or I should say both, since only Agathon and Socrates are left.

Oh, I'll go along with you, Eryximachus declared, since your speech delighted me so much. And if I didn't know that Socrates and Agathon were masters of erotica, I would be afraid that they'd be at a loss for words after all the myriad of things that have been said! However, I'm thoroughly confident.

Then Socrates spoke up. That's fine for you, Eryximachus, you did so well. But if you were where I am now, or rather, where I shall be after Agathon has spoken eloquently, you would be quite fearful, exactly as I am now!

You want to bewitch me, Socrates, said Agathon, so that I'll be disturbed by thinking that the audience has great expectations about my eloquence.

I would certainly be forgetful, Agathon, replied Socrates, if knowing your manliness and greatness of mind when you presented yourself on stage with your actors, and faced that great audience squarely without the slightest perturbation, for the production of your work, I believed now that you could be upset by our little group of people.

But Socrates, exclaimed Agathon, Do you think I'm so blown up by the theater that I don't know that anyone with intelligence is more afraid of a few intelligent men than a multitude of fools?

I'd not do you the slightest justice, Agathon, Socrates allowed, if I thought you were naive. I know very well that when you meet people you consider intelligent, you think much more of them than of the masses. But, suppose we aren't like them—after all, we were present there, we made up part of the crowd—but if you were to meet others, wise men, surely you would be ashamed before them if you

D thought you were actually doing something shameful. . . . Isn't that so?

True enough, he agreed.

But you wouldn't mind before the crowd—if you thought you were doing something shameful?

Phaedrus, he says, broke in here—Agathon, my friend, if you answer Socrates it won't matter to him any more what happens to our project here, as long as he gets somebody to argue with him—particularly if that body is a beauty to boot! Personally, I'm delighted to listen to Socrates' arguments, but I am responsible for superintending this encomium to Love, and I must receive a speech from each of you. Both of you must pay up and give your dissertations to the god!

E Ah, you're quite right, Phaedrus, Agathon declared, and nothing is going to get in the way of my speaking. There'll be plenty of time for me to argue with Socrates later.

Agathon

First I'd like to say how I should speak, then make my speech. It seems to me that none of the other speakers have praised the god, but have celebrated men for the joys of which the god is the source. About the nature of the one who has 195 bestowed these blessings, no one has spoken. There is one proper mode for every paean, in every case: The nature of the subject of the speech—whoever that may be—and of the things he causes, should succeed in coming through in the speech. So that it seems to me only just to discuss first the nature of the god Love, and then his gifts.

I declare, then, if I may speak without censure or reproach, that of all the gods, those joyful ones, Love is the most joyful, most beautiful, best.

He is so beautiful in that, first, Phaedrus, he is the very B youngest of the gods. He himself provides sure proof for this assertion, running for refuge from old age (a quick thing, obviously—it overtakes us far more quickly than it should). Indeed, Love instinctively loathes it, and avoids it even at a distance. On the other hand, he is always with the young, and is so, as well, for the old saying holds well, that like likes like.

Whereas I agree with Phaedrus in many cases, I can't accept that statement that Love is older than Cronos and Iapetus. I say he is the youngest of the gods, and always

c young, and that the ancient acts of the gods, of which Hesiod and Parmenides tell, were done by Necessity, and not by Love; that is, if those writers tell the truth. They would not have castrated or enchained one another, nor done the many other violent things, if Love had been among them. But affection and peace, by which Love rules the gods, would have prevailed, as they do now.

So, you see, he is young, and tender in his youth. It de-mands a poet such as Homer to describe the exquisite tender-

d ness of this god. Homer speaks of Delusion as a goddess, and of her tenderness—how tender her feet were—singing:

Her feet are tender; for not upon the earth does
she come, but see, she treads upon the heads of men.

There it seems to me this sweetest tenderness is manifest in a beautiful testimony, for she does not tread upon stiff stuff,

e but upon soft. And in the same way we would employ a testament to the tenderness of Love. For he doesn't come upon the earth, nor, for that matter, upon our heads, which are not at all soft, but it is in the very softest parts of living things that he comes, and lives. In the characters and souls of gods and men he embeds himself, but it should be added, not in all souls. When he finds the character of a person to be hard, he abandons him, but when he finds it soft, he will dwell there.

Thus clinging always, feet and all, in the very softest souls

196 of gentle men, he must surely be the tenderest of things.

Youngest, surely, and tenderest, and in addition, supple in form. He would not be the god who enfolds all things, he would not escape, going in at first, then going out of every heart, if he were stiff.

Of the symmetry and suppleness of his form, his grace provides strong testimony; that grace which all agree Love possesses beyond everyone, for Love without grace is simply a contradiction in terms.

B   The beauty of his skin shines for the life he lives in flowers. In a body or soul, or anything else that is withered or past its bloom, Love will not stay, but if a place is fragrant and filled with blossoms, there he will stop and stay.

Of the beauties, then, of our god, enough has been said, although there is still much left. But I shall go on to speak of the goodness of Love.

His greatness is that he treats no god or man unjustly, nor is he unjustly treated by any god, or man. He himself does
C   not suffer violence—if acted on at all—violence cannot apply to Love. Nor when he acts, does he act with violence, for in all ways men all serve Love with willing hearts, and the things one does of one's own free will, by voluntary covenant, *the sovereign of our state—the laws*—declares to be just.

And beyond his justice he is filled with temperance. For we define temperance as the control of pleasure and desire, and no pleasure is more powerful than Love. If they are weaker, Love will control and they will be controlled, and controlling pleasures and desires, Love would be especially temperate!

D   Further, *not even Ares can resist* the courage of Love. Ares doesn't capture Love, but Love—of Aphrodite—does catch Ares, as the story goes. The captor is more powerful than the captured, and if he overcomes one who is braver than all others, he must be the bravest.

Thus, the justice, the temperance and the courage of the god have been described and only his wisdom is left. As far as I am able, I will try not to slight it.

First, that I may honor my art, as Eryximachus did his:

E our god is a poet, so masterful as to make others poets as well. At least, everyone becomes a poet, *however songless he may have been before*, once Love takes hold of him. Which is fitting for us to take as proof that Love is a gifted poet, in

197 short, of every expressive art. For the things one doesn't have or know about, one can't give another, or teach. And I ask you, who could deny that the creation of all living things is anything but the art of Love, by which all animate things come to be and develop? On the other hand, do we not know that a craftsman for whom this god has been the teacher becomes celebrated and brilliant, while when Love has not taken hold of one, he remains obscure? Archery, certainly, and medicine, and divination, Apollo invented, under the influence of desire and Love, so that he too is a student of

B Love. So too, the Muses, when they discovered music, and Hephaestus, when he invented the smith's art, and Athene, weaving, and even Zeus, *the government of gods and men*. From which, too, it is obvious that those acts of the gods were contrived when Love was being born—the love, that is, of beauty—because there is nothing ugly about Love. Before this, however, as I said at the outset, the gods did many awful things, or so they say, under the compulsion of Necessity; but then this god was born, and from then on the ability to love beauty has created all the good things that exist for gods and men.

C So Love himself seems to me, Phaedrus, the most beautiful and the very best of the gods—and beyond that to be the source of all the other qualities of this type in others. A desire has come over me just now to make up a poem about the way he creates:

> Peace among men, a calm stillness to the sea, rest for the winds, and for human sorrow, sleep.

D He empties out feelings of alienation, and fills us with intimacy, brings us together in all such relations with one another as this—in festivals, in dances, at sacrificial rites, where he himself becomes the leader. He bestows gentleness, banishing brutality, loves to give joy while withholding grief, and has a graceful cheerfulness. Wise men may look at him, and the gods find him wonderful. By those who are unhappy he is coveted, by those who have a happy lot, treasured. He is the begetter of delicacy and elegance, wantonness and beneficence, of human desire and yearning. He is

E concerned with good men, mindless of bad. In misery, in fear, in drunkenness and the affairs of state, shipmate, comrade, and dearest savior, ornament of all gods and men together, most beautiful and highest leader, whom all men must follow, singing sweetly and partaking of the music he sings as he enchants the mind of every god and man.

And this, he concluded, is the speech I offer, Phaedrus, in dedication to the god. It is partly in a light and partly in a serious mode, combined with all the skill I have.

198 At Agathon's saying this, reported Aristodemus, the people who were there applauded this speech which so became the young man who had given it, as well as the god! Then Socrates spoke, looking at Eryximachus.

Doesn't it seem to you, oh son of Acumenus, he started out, that I wasn't afraid without cause back there, or was I not speaking like a prophet when I predicted that Agathon would talk brilliantly and that I'd be at a complete loss?

Well, said Eryximachus, I agree that you were prophetic

B in saying that Agathon would speak well; I very much doubt if you are at a loss.

But how, my good friend, Socrates said, could I not be at a loss for words—I or anyone else, for that matter, when I'm expected to follow such a beautiful, many-faceted speech as has just been delivered? The rest of it was not quite so amazing, but that part at the end—who, hearing the beauty of those words and phrases, wouldn't have been astounded?

C I would have run away and escaped from shame when I realized that I would not be able to speak nearly as well, if I'd had somewhere else to go!

The speech reminded me of Gorgias—and I felt exactly

like Homer's character. I was afraid that, in his conclusion, Agathon would hold up to me the awesome Gorgias' head, in opposing his oration to mine, and strike me as voiceless as stone! Then I realized how ridiculous it was to have agreed to take my turn along with you in praising Love, and to have

D   said that I was an expert in love-matters, without knowing how one ought to speak in praise. To begin with, I stupidly thought one ought to speak the truth about anything which is being eulogized; and having this as a foundation, the speaker could esteem the most beautiful aspects and present them in the most becoming manner. So I was thinking to my-self how really beautifully I would speak, since I knew the truth. But now it looks as if this is not what it means to dis-

E   cuss something "beautifully," but rather one should ascribe the greatest and most beautiful qualities to it, whether it has them or not. If it is false, it doesn't matter. It was ar-ranged beforehand, it seems, that each of us should appear to praise Love, but that we should not really praise him. That's why, I believe, you dredged up all those sayings and applied them to Love, declaring him such and such, and the cause of such and such, so that he could be described as 'most

199 beautiful' and 'best,' and obviously for people who don't know him—for this wouldn't work with people who know, however beautiful and awesome the eulogy may be! But I didn't realize that this was to be the way the praises would be given, and I ignorantly agreed to offer my praises in turn. *The tongue, yes,* as they say, *but not the heart.* Really—I want out! I'll never make a speech of praise that way! I'm

B   not capable of it! If you like, I'm willing to speak only the truth, in my own style, and not in competition with your own dissertations, so that I'm not branded a laughing-stock. So look here, Phaedrus, do you want a speech like this— do you want to listen to an honest description of Love, with the words and phrases of the sentiments expressed in just the form and order that they happen to come along?

Then he said that Phaedrus and the others commanded him

to speak in whatever way he felt he had to address them.

But furthermore, he said, allow me to question Agathon a bit, Phaedrus, so that I can come to some agreement with him before I speak.

C   Oh, I'll give way, answered Phaedrus. Go ahead and question him. And so it was after this sort of stuff that our friend Socrates began at this point.

Agathon & Socrates

Now, Agathon my friend, it seems to me that you led off your discussion beautifully by saying that it is necessary first to show what the nature of Love is, and then to discuss his works. I thoroughly admire such a beginning. So tell me this about Love please, since the rest of what you said about him was so beautiful and splendid—is Love such as to be the love of something, or of nothing? I'm not asking if it is the love of some mother or father—to ask whether Love is the love of a mother or father would be absurd—but as if I were asking about a father. Is a father the father of someone, or not? You should undoubtedly say to me, if you wanted to answer me properly, that it is of a son or daughter that a father is a father. Or wouldn't you?

Certainly, said Agathon.

And it would be the same for a mother?

They were in agreement about that as well.

E   But now then, continued Socrates, answer a few more, so that you get a better understanding of what I want. Let me ask you this: a brother—the thing itself, just as it is—is it the brother of someone or not?

He answered that it was.

Is it not, then, the brother of a brother or sister?

Yes.

So try, he went on, and tell me about Love. Is Love the love of nothing or of something?

200   Surely he is the love of something!

Now think, Socrates urged, of what this may be, and keep
it to yourself; but tell me whether he desires this thing of
which Love is the love or not?

Oh yes, Agathon replied.

Does he have the thing which he desires and loves, when
he desires and loves it, or does he not have it?

He doesn't have it, I would guess, Agathon said.

Then consider, continued Socrates, beyond guessing,
B   whether it isn't necessary for the desiring thing to desire what
is lacking, and not to desire it if it isn't lacking? It seems
marvelously clear to me, Agathon, that this is necessary.
What about you?

It seems that way to me, too, he said.

Good. So, would anyone wish to be great when he was
great? Or strong if he were strong?

That would be impossible, from what we've been saying.

Since they would not be lacking that which they were.

True.

For if he were strong, and still should want to be strong,
said Socrates, or swift, and wanted to be swift, or healthy,
and wanted to be healthy—since one generally thinks in that
C   sort of situation, and in all of the same sorts of cases, that
those who are of such and such a nature and possess those
same qualities, want the things that they have (I'm inserting
this so that we won't deceive ourselves), for these men,
Agathon, if you think about it, it is imperative that they have
everything, at a given moment, which they have, whether
they wish it or not, and who, I ask you, would desire that?
But whenever someone says 'I am healthy, and I want to be
healthy,' 'I am rich, and I want to be rich,' or 'I desire the
D   very things I have,' we shall say to him, 'you mean, dear
fellow, that possessing riches, health and strength, you want
to possess them in the future, too, since as far as the present is
concerned you have them, desiring it or not.' But look, when
you say 'I desire my present belongings,' do you think you're

saying anything besides: 'I wish that the things I have now will be provided for me in the future?' Wouldn't he agree?

Certainly, said Agathon.

Then Socrates went on, So there is a love of that which is not present for one, which one doesn't have, namely the existence of those things in the future, preserved, and provided always.

Absolutely, he answered.

E   Now such a person, and every other person who feels longing, longs for what is not at hand, for what he isn't himself, and for what he lacks, and these are the sorts of thing that desire is of, and Love?

Definitely, he said.

So come, urged Socrates, let us agree on what has been said. Is Love, first of all, anything but the love of things? And further, isn't it of those very things which it needs?

That's right, Agathon agreed.

201   Indeed, now think back to the things you said about Love in your oration. If you like, I'll remind you. I believe you spoke of the way that the deeds of the gods were initiated because of the love of beautiful things. For there couldn't be a love of ugly things. Didn't you say that?

Yes, I said it, replied Agathon.

And you spoke quite properly, my friend, asserted Socrates. And if this is the case, can Love be the love of anything but beauty, and not ugliness?

He granted that.

B   Then wasn't it agreed that he loves what he lacks and doesn't have?

Yes, he said.

Love, then, is wanting in beauty, and doesn't have it?

Necessarily.

But what have we here? Would you say that what was wanting in beauty and in no way possesses beauty was beautiful?

Obviously, it isn't.

Are you then still going to agree that Love is beautiful, if that's how it is?

And Agathon declared, I'm afraid, Socrates, that I didn't know what I was talking about.

C   Oh, but you spoke beautifully, Agathon, he assured him. But tell me a little more. Don't you think of what is good as being beautiful as well?

Yes, I do.

Then again—if Love is lacking in beauty, and the good is beautiful, he must be lacking in goodness as well.

Socrates! he exclaimed, I'm incapable of refuting you, so have it your own way!

D   The truth, lovely Agathon, Socrates said, you cannot refute, but Socrates is easily refuted.

Socrates & Diotima

But I'm going to leave you alone now, and give the account concerning Love which I once heard from a woman of Mantinea, Diotima, who was wise about such things and many others as well. It was she who once gave the Athenians a ten-year respite from disease, by getting them to make sacrifices against the plague. She was my teacher about Love, and I shall try to relate for you, using the points on which Agathon and I agreed, in my own words, and as well as I can,

E   what she told me. It is necessary, Agathon, just as you have indicated, for one to define Love first, and describe his nature, and then to go on to his works. I think it would be easiest for me to follow the procedure the foreign woman used when she questioned me then. I was saying to her pretty nearly the same things that you were to me just now, Agathon—that Love was a great god, and was of beautiful things. So she questioned me on these propositions, just the way I've done here, showing that according to my theory he couldn't be either beautiful or good.

How can you say that, Diotima? I demanded. Can Love then be ugly and evil?

But she said, Be quiet! Do you think that whatever isn't beautiful must necessarily be ugly?

202 Absolutely.

And that anyone who isn't wise, is ignorant? Or don't you realize that there is something in between wisdom and ignorance?

What is that?

Don't you know, she said: having correct opinions without being able to explain them. That isn't knowledge (for how can something without reason be knowledge?) but it's not ignorance, either (if one chances on what really is, how can that be ignorance?). But correct opinion has just this quality: it is between understanding and ignorance.

And I had to agree that there was truth in what she was saying.

B Then don't insist on the thing which isn't beautiful being ugly, or on the thing which isn't good being evil. And when you can bring yourself to agree that Love is neither good nor beautiful, it won't be necessary anymore for him to be ugly and evil. Rather he is between these, she said.

But everyone agrees that Love is a great god, I argued.

Do you mean every ignorant one, she countered, or every knowledgeable one?

I mean *everyone!*

C Here she laughed. And how, Socrates, can those people agree that he is such a great god, who deny his being a god at all?

Who are they? I asked.

You, she declared, for one, and me for another!

And I demanded, How is that? Socrates said.

It's simple, she continued. Tell me, wouldn't you say that all gods are joyous and beautiful? Or do you presume to deny the beauty and happiness of the gods?

Not I, by god! I exclaimed.

And wouldn't you say that those who are happy are those who have good and beautiful things?

Completely so.

But you have just now agreed that Love, in his want of good and beautiful things, yearns after the things of which he is in need.

Yes, I did agree to that.

But how, I ask you, could he be a god when he hasn't any share of beautiful and good things?

No, that doesn't seem at all possible.

Then you can see, she asserted, that you are ruling Love a nongod?

But, I asked, what is Love then? A mortal?

Not in the least!

But what then?

Like those things we first discussed—he is intermediate between mortal and immortal.

What is such a thing, Diotima?

A great daemon, Socrates. The entire world of the daemonic is intermediate between divinity and mortality.

What power does it possess? I asked.

Interpreting and communicating human affairs to the gods and divine matters to men—the prayers and sacrifices of men, and the commands and responses of the gods. Being in the middle, it fulfills both, and in this way unites the whole with itself. Through this intermediary all divination proceeds,
and religious practice involving sacrifices, mystery rites, magical incantations, all enchantments and sorcery. A god doesn't have intercourse with a human being, but all mingling and dialogue between gods and men take place through this intermediary, both in wakefulness and in dreams. One who knows of such things is a daemonic man, while one who is versed in any other skill, be it craft or any handiwork, is just a workman. Actually, there are many of these daemons, and they are of all kinds, and Love is one of them.

But his father—who was that? And his mother? I asked.

B   That's a rather long story to recount, she answered, but I'll
tell it to you. When Aphrodite was born, the gods were
feasting, a group of them, including the son of Invention,
Resource. And when they had dined, Poverty came along
begging since there was a party going on. So she stood
there at the doors. Now Resource, having gotten quite
drunk on nectar—there was no wine then—had gone out to
Zeus' little garden, and in his discomfort fallen asleep. Here
Poverty schemed, since she herself was without resource, to
C   have a child by Resource; and she lay with him and thereby
conceived Love. For this reason Love has been Aphrodite's
attendant and servant, because he was conceived on the day
of her birth, and at the same time is by nature a lover of
beauty because of Aphrodite's being so beautiful.

Therefore, as the son of Resource and Poverty, Love finds
himself in this situation: first of all, he is always impover-
D   ished, and far from being tender and beautiful, as most people
think, he is harsh and rugged, barefoot and homeless; always
lying unsheltered on the ground, he is lulled to sleep on
doorsteps and in the open roads. Possessing his mother's
nature, he is always in need. But, then again, through his father he turns out a schemer for beautiful and good things,
is courageous, bold, and intense, an awesome hunter always
devising some machination or other, eager for understanding
and inventive; he is a lover of wisdom throughout his life,
E   and a brilliant wizard, healer and philosopher!

And so he was born neither immortal nor mortal. In one
day, then, when he is happy, he will spring into life, and then
will die, but once again be brought back to life through his
father's nature! But his power is always ebbing away, so that
Love is never utterly at a loss nor completely wealthy. He
exists in the middle, between wisdom and ignorance. It is like
204   this: no god desires wisdom or longs to become wise—they
are that—nor does anyone else who is wise desire wisdom. But
then those who are ignorant don't desire wisdom or long to
become wise either. That's exactly the problem with igno-

rance—a person who lacks beauty and goodness and intelligence seems perfectly satisfactory to himself. A person who doesn't think of himself as lacking anything won't desire what he doesn't think he lacks!

Then who, Diotima, I asked, are the lovers of wisdom, if it's not wise or ignorant men?

B   It would be obvious, she answered, even to a child, that it is the ones who are intermediate between them both—and Love is one of these. Wisdom is certainly one of the most beautiful things, and Love is the love of what is beautiful. By necessity, then, Love is a lover of wisdom, a philosopher, and as a philosopher, is intermediate between the wise and the ignorant. And the cause of these facts, again, is his birth. Because on the one hand his father was wise and fortunate, while his mother was unwise and resourceless.

This, then, dear Socrates, is the very nature of a daemon.

C   But it's not remarkable that you came to think of Love the way you did. I believe I may infer from what you said that you imagined Love was the beloved, not the loving. For this reason Love appeared to you, I suppose, as utterly beautiful. For, in fact, it is the beloved that is beautiful and delicate, perfect and most blessed. But that which feels love takes a different form, just as I've explained.

And I answered: Amen, you remarkable woman! You put that so well! But if Love is of such a nature, what function does he serve for men?

D   That's exactly what I shall try to teach you next, Socrates, she said. To begin with, Love's nature and birth are just as I've said, but then too, he is "of beautiful things," as you've put it. But suppose someone were to ask us: 'What is the Love of beautiful things, Socrates and Diotima?' Or, let me state it more clearly: 'If one loves beautiful things, what is this love?'

And I replied that it was that they would become one's own.

But this answer, she went on, demands a further question,

such as: 'Once these beautiful things have become a person's, what will he have?'

I have absolutely nothing at hand, I said, to offer as an answer to such a question.

E   But, she continued, supposing one substituted 'the good' for 'the beautiful' and put the question: 'Look, Socrates, I say to you, what does someone who loves good things love?'

Their becoming his, I answered.

And what does the fellow have who gets these good things?

That's easier, I responded. I can answer that he has joy.

205   So, she concluded, by the possession of good things, happy people are happy, and there is no longer any need to ask why a man who wishes for happiness, wishes it. Rather, this answer seems to be complete.

Very true, I asserted.

But do you think that such a desire and love are really common to all men, and that they all desire good things for themselves? What do you say?

Yes, I said. It is common to all.

B   How is it then, Socrates, she asked, that we don't say that all men love, if all men do always love the same things? Rather we say that some men love, while others do not.

I'm puzzled by that myself, I replied.

Don't puzzle over it, she said. What happens is that we take a certain form of love and call that 'love,' which is the name of the whole; and we misuse the names of other things, too.

Like what, I asked.

For instance, you know that *poetry** is very diverse: that

C   the entire process of turning a thing from nonbeing into being, is poetry, that all kinds of work involving all sorts of

---

* Diotima says ποίησις, a word which means simply a making, fabrication, production and thus *creation* in general. Even when the word was used in the more restricted sense in which it is generally understood, this wider connotation remained as an underlying presence. (Translator's note.)

techniques are poetry, and that the craftsmen who do the work on them are all "poets."

This is true.

In the same way you know, she went on, that they aren't all called 'poets,' but have other names, and from the whole of poetry one part is selected—that which is concerned with music and meter—and this is called by the name of the whole. By *poetry* is meant that alone, and those who do this sort of poetry are called 'poets.'

Yes, it's true, I agreed.

So, it's the same way, you see, regarding love. In its generic aspect love is the entire desire for good things, and for the happiness they give,

> *most powerful and all ensnaring Love.*

But those who turn to him in his many other aspects, either in trade, or love of gymnastic exercise, or philosophy, these aren't said to be aspects of love, nor are the people called 'lovers.' However, those who go after the one specific aspect, and court it, they get the name of the whole—they are said to be lovers and to love.

It's very likely that what you say is true, I said.

Whereas a person might make up a story, she continued, that those who seek after the other halves of themselves are loving, my own account describes love as being neither of the half nor of the whole, unless it should chance, my friend, to be something good, since men are ready to have their own hands and feet cut off if it seems to them that these things are harmful to them! No one cherishes what is his own for its own sake, I believe, unless one were to call that which belongs to one 'good' and that which is foreign 'evil.' So that what men love is nothing other than the good. Don't you think so?

By god, I do! I exclaimed.

Then, she asked, may we say simply that what men love is the good?

Yes, I agreed.

But then, she said, shouldn't we add that they desire the good to be theirs?

Yes, let that be added.

Then, furthermore, not only to be theirs, but to be so forever?

Yes, add that too.

To put it briefly, love is for the good to always belong to oneself.

Absolutely true! I declared.

B Since love is always of this nature, she went on, how is it pursued? How does this zeal and vehemence find its way into actions? How does it actually work? Can you say?

I wouldn't marvel so at you, Diotima, I replied, and at your wisdom, and attend your teachings to learn these very things, if I could.

Then I'll tell you, she assured me. It is procreation in a beautiful thing—of the body and of the soul.

One would need a prophet to comprehend what you're saying.

C All right, she responded, I'll put it more clearly. You see, Socrates, all humans are pregnant, physically and spiritually, and when we reach our prime, our nature desires to give birth. Nature is not capable of giving birth in the ugly, but only in the beautiful. Now this is a divine act, and this pregnancy and birth impart immortality to a living being who is

D mortal. But it is impossible for these things to come about in the unharmonious. The ugly clashes with all that is divine, while beauty is in harmony with it. Therefore the role of the goddess of childbirth is played by beauty. And because of this, whenever something pregnant approaches the beautiful it becomes gentle and pours out gladness both in the begetting and the birth. But whenever it approaches the ugly, it shrinks into itself, sullen and upset. It turns away, is repelled, and refuses to give birth. It holds back and carries the burden of what it has inside itself with pain. In fact, within the

E   pregnant one, who is teeming with life, there is a violent fluttering before the beautiful, through which it will be released from the great pain of childbirth which it has. But love is not, Socrates, she cautioned, a love of the beautiful, as you may believe.

But of what then?

Of giving birth and procreation in the beautiful.

Is that it, then?

Absolutely, she replied. And why is it of giving birth? Because giving birth is the eternal and immortal element in

207   the mortal, and it's necessary to desire immortality along with the good, from what we've agreed—that love is for the good to be eternally one's own. So, really, from this same assumption it necessarily follows that love is of immortality.

All these ideas, then, she taught me, when she would discourse on love. And once she asked,

What do you believe, Socrates, to be the source of this love, this desire? Look—don't you perceive how profoundly it moves all wild beasts, footed and winged, when they desire

B   to procreate? How they all become sick and deranged with love, at first with the desire for intercourse with one another, and then for nourishing their offspring? How the weakest ones are prepared to fight against the strongest, and to die? How these beasts will wear themselves down with hunger so as to feed their children, and to do anything else that's necessary? A person might imagine, she suggested, that human

C   beings do these things out of rationality. But what causes the wild beasts to be so deeply moved by love? What can you say?

And I replied that I didn't know.

She asked then: Do you intend to become a master in matters concerning love when you don't understand these things?

But that's exactly why I came to you, Diotima, as I said before. I realized my need for instruction. Please, explain the cause of these and any other things that arise because of love.

D Well, she answered, if you believe that love has the nature
we have often agreed on, you shouldn't wonder. In this case
the story is the same as that one—mortal nature always seeks
as much as it can to exist forever and achieve immortality.
But it is able to do this only by means of procreation, its way
of always leaving behind another, young one, against old
age. It is particularly in this that each living individual is said
to be alive and to be itself—just as one is described as oneself and the same person from childhood until becoming old.
But in actuality one hasn't any characteristics at all whereby
one can be called the same person. One is always becoming a
E new person, losing things, portions of hair, flesh, bones, blood
and all the stuff of the body. And not only in the body. In
the soul as well one's habits and character, beliefs, desires,
pleasures, pains, fears—none of these things remain the same
in anyone—they arise and they die out. But what's even
208 stranger than these facts is that we not only gain knowledge
and lose it, so that we don't remain the same people with
respect to what we know, but that every single example of
knowledge suffers the same thing! For a man is said to study
when there is a departing of knowledge. Forgetting is a
leaving of knowledge, and study, by implanting new knowledge in place of what has left, saves the memory of it, so that
it seems like the same thing. It is in this way that everything
mortal is preserved—not by its being utterly the same forever,
B like the divine, but by what is old and withdrawing leaving
behind something else, something new, like itself. It is by this
method, Socrates, that the mortal partakes of immortality,
she explained, in the body and in all other respects. It is not
possible any other way. On account of this, it is not surprising if everything, by nature, honors its own progeny, for
in all, the same intensity and love seeks the joy of immortality.

When I heard this argument I was amazed, and said, Is it
C possible, wise Diotima, that such things are really true?

And she, just like those precious professors, said, Know it

well, Socrates! You might be amazed at the unreasonableness
of what I've told you if you looked at the ambitions of men,
unless you considered how terribly, in their love, they are
affected by a desire to acquire a name,

and to store away fame for all immortal time,

and for the sake of this are prepared to run all risks, greater
even than those they run for their children: to go through

D their wealth, to suffer pains of all sorts, and even to sacrifice
their lives! Do you imagine, she asked, that Alcestis would
have died for Admetus, or Achilles would have sought death
for Patroclus, or our own Codrus would have welcomed
death for the sake of his children's kingdom, unless they believed that they were securing for themselves *the undying
memory of virtue*, which we now hold? Certainly not, she

E said. I believe they all performed all their renowned deeds for
the sake of the immortality of virtue and such a reputation,
and the more so to the degree that they are better people.
For they desire the immortal. However, those who are pro-
lific, she said, when they are so in body, turn in preference to
women and in this way are their lovers, so that through the
conception of children they achieve immortality, memory
and joy, and they believe that they are *providing all things*

209 *against a future time* for themselves. But when it's in the soul
—for there are some people who are pregnant more in their
souls than in their bodies, with things which are fitting for
the soul to bear and bring to life. And what is fitting in this
way? Thought—and other virtue. Of these things, you see, all
poets are progenitors, and those craftsmen who are said to
be inventors. And by far the greatest, she asserted, and most
beautiful part of thought is that which concerns the ordering

B of cities and households, whose name is wisdom* and justice.

---

* The Greek word σωφροσύνη (sophrosyne) is one for which
there is no true English equivalent. It is usually translated "temperance," but that word has taken on connotations in English

Whenever a person is filled with these things from his youth, so as to be divine in his soul, when he becomes a man he yearns to bring forth and beget, and goes around seeking, I believe, for the beautiful thing in which he can generate. For he cannot generate in an ugly thing. And so, being pregnant with these things, he welcomes beautiful bodies rather than ugly ones, and if he should chance on a soul who has beauty of nature and body, he delights greatly in both together, and immediately indulges in talks with this man about

c   virtue, and about the sort of person that a good man must be, and about what things are properly done by him. He is taking his education in hand. For I believe that when he fastens onto this beautiful person and has intercourse with him, he gives birth to the things he has been carrying up to then, and brings them to life when, present or absent, he thinks about him. He then nurtures what has been conceived together with that person. Such men share an intimacy with one another which is far deeper than one coming from children and enjoy a surer affection, because they have taken part in the creation of more beautiful and immortal progeny!

---

which are inappropriate to the Greek meaning. Sophrosyne is a quality of character which combines temperance and moderation with a sense of proportion and a degree of self-control which is neither too rigid for the health of the individual nor too indeterminate to do him any good. It is that quality one finds in people who are able to value things in their proper proportions; who are capable of warmth, excitement, and enjoyment as well as of seriousness, intensity, and grief, all in the right measure and in proper relation to the events and situations experienced. It is the ability to know what is genuinely important and to respond appropriately. As there is no single word in English which conveys this quality with all its subtle implications, it has seemed that a number of different renderings, each suitable to the context in which the word occurs, would give the reader a less distorted sense of the original idea than a single, consistent translation which is inappropriate to the shifting connotations of the Greek concept. (Translator's note.)

Everyone would choose for himself to give birth to these
D   sorts of children rather than human ones! Men look at Homer
and Hesiod and the other great poets and are jealous of the
kind of offspring they left behind them, because they are
the kind of beings which afford to those men a deathless fame
and memory. Or, if you like, she went on, Lycurgus, the
savior of Lacedaemonia, and, as it were, all Hellas, left behind
such children in Lacedaemonia. And Solon, too, is more
honored by you on account of his creation of the laws; and
E   other men too, in many other places, among the Greeks and
barbarians alike, men who are the producers of many beautiful works, bringing forth every sort of virtue. Many shrines
have been instituted for them because of the sort of children
they had, while for the sake of human ones there is not one.

It is these kinds of mysteries about love, Socrates, into
210   which you may perhaps be initiated. I don't know if you are
the sort of man to grasp the higher mysteries, the end to
which these lead if correctly followed. But, she promised,
I'll tell you about them, and I'll not spare any effort on my
own part. You must try to follow as best you can.

It is necessary, she asserted, for one who is going to proceed to this goal properly, to begin as a young man by being
drawn to the beauty of the body, and if he is being guided
properly by his guide, to love the beauty of one body, and
B   for the fruit of this love to be beautiful conversations. But
then this man must perceive that the beauty of one particular body is related to the beauty of another body, and if
he must pursue beauty of form it is utterly senseless not to
consider as one and the same the beauty which exists in all
bodies. Once he has understood this, he will become a lover
of all beautiful bodies, but he'll despise his lust for the one,
and give it up, considering it petty. After this, he will find
the beauty that exists in souls more valuable than that in the
body, so that when there is decency of soul in someone,
although this person may have very little of the bloom of
C   physical beauty, it satisfies him to love him and care for him

and to beget with him the sort of conversations that make
young men better, so that he is compelled further to contemplate the beauty which exists in daily pursuits, and laws,
and to see here too, how each kind of beauty is related, so
that he will come to consider physical beauty rather a minor
thing. After actions one comes to kinds of knowledge, so that
one sees the beauty of the sciences, and gazing now at this

D   vast beauty, one can no longer be the low, petty slave of an
isolated instance of beauty, cherishing, like a lackey, the
beauty of a young boy, or of some one person, or even of a
single activity. One turns and contemplates the great sea of
beauty; one brings forth many beautiful and magnificent
theories and thoughts in a fruitful philosophy, until, growing
strong and thriving in this environment, he comprehends a
certain single knowledge, which is of this kind of beauty—

E   now you must try, she interjected, to keep your mind with
me as well as you can—the man who has been instructed, up
to this point, in an understanding of matters of love, looking
at beauty in correct and orderly succession, when he comes
to the end of these love matters will suddenly behold a thing
which is miraculously beautiful by nature! It is this very
thing, Socrates, for the sake of which all the earlier hardships

211 were suffered. First of all, it is eternal, and neither comes
into being nor perishes, neither waxes nor wanes. Then it is
not beautiful in part and ugly in part, nor beautiful at one
time and ugly at another, nor beautiful in relation to one
thing and ugly in relation to another, nor is it beautiful from
one point of view but ugly from another (so that to some
it is beautiful while it is ugly to others). Furthermore, the
Beautiful will not manifest itself to this man as a face or pair
of hands, or any other bodily thing; nor in any proposition,
or science, nor as existing anywhere in something else, such

B   as an animal, or the earth or the heavens, or any other thing
whatever. It exists by itself in itself, eternally, and in one
form only, and all other beautiful things participate in it in
such a way that, while they come into being and perish, it

does not, nor does it become greater or less, nor is it affected by anything.

So, whenever someone, making his way from these kinds c of beauties, through the correct use of his love for boys, begins to behold this, the Beautiful in itself, he has pretty much attained the ultimate end. This is what it means to progress correctly to an understanding of matters of love, or to be brought to it by another: in beginning from these sorts of beauties, to move up constantly for the sake of that beauty (as if he were using the steps of a stair), from one to two, and from two to all beautiful bodies, from beautiful bodies to beautiful acts, from beautiful acts to the beauties of learning, from learning finally to that knowledge which is none other than knowledge of the Beautiful itself, so that he comes to D know, in the end, what beauty is. Here above all places, my dear Socrates, said the woman from far-off Mantinea, is the life that is worth living for a man, lived in the contemplation of the Beautiful itself. If you ever do see this, it will seem to you to be very different from the gold or clothing or beautiful boys and youths you now look at with amazement, so that you are ready, like so many others, when you are looking at your darlings and always being with them, to give up eating and drinking (if such a thing were possible), and E only gaze on at them and make love! How would it be, let us imagine, if someone could see the Beautiful itself, pure, clear, unmixed—not infected with human flesh and color, and a lot of other mortal nonsense—if he were able to know the 212 divinely Beautiful itself, in its unique form? Do you think, she went on, that the life of a man who could look in that way, who could contemplate that entity, and live with it by means of the proper faculty, would be meaningless? Don't you realize, she asked, that only there, seeing in the way that the Beautiful can be seen, can one stop giving birth to images of virtue, since one no longer holds on to images, but to truth, because one now grasps the truth? He is able to bring forth true virtue, and to nourish it, and hence to be a favorite of the gods, so that if any man can be immortal, it will be he.

B   So, Phaedrus, and the rest of you, that is what Diotima told me, and I am persuaded. And because I do believe in it I would like to try and persuade others that for a nature like the human one, we cannot easily find a better helper toward the possession of such a life, than Love. That is why I assert that every man ought to honor Love, as I myself do honor him, devoting myself assiduously to matters of love and urging others to do the same. Now and always, I praise the

C   power and courage of Love as much as I can. So, Phaedrus, consider this story, if you will, as my encomium, spoken in praise of Love. If you will not, please call it whatever you are disposed to call it.

When Socrates had finished speaking they applauded, and Aristophanes started to say something about how Socrates, in his speech, had made reference to his own. Then, suddenly, there was a terrific din—a banging on the door that led to the courtyard—like drunkards—and they heard the music of

D   a flute-girl. At this point Agathon called out: Attendants, won't you go and see who it is? If it's one of our friends, invite him in, and if it isn't say we're not drinking, we're all finished.

In no time at all they heard the voice of Alcibiades out in the hall—shouting out loud—extremely drunk—asking where was Agathon—ordering them to take him to Agathon! So between them they brought him in, with the flute-girl lending support from underneath, with several others of his

E   followers as well, and he stood there at the door, garlanded with ivy and violets in a thick wreath and fillets all about his head in great profusion. And he said:

Gracious Gentlemen: Will you accept this fellow as a drinking partner? I am totally and utterly drunk! Or shall I simply crown Agathon with a wreath—as I came to do—and go away? I couldn't get here yesterday, you see, he continued, so I've come now with these fillets around my head—

I want to take them off my own—this brilliant, most beautiful fellow—if I may say it—I want to tie them on his head— 213 you're laughing at me for being drunk like this? You may laugh all you like—all the same, I know perfectly well that I'm talking honestly. But tell me at once!—on the terms I stated—will you drink with me, or not?

Then they all cried out in acclaim, and demanded that he come in and get comfortable, and Agathon called him over. With his people leading him he went in, undid the fillets which had been tied around his head, so that they were over his eyes and he couldn't see Socrates, and sat down beside

B Agathon—between Socrates and his host (for Socrates had moved aside when he saw Alcibiades). So, he sat down there, embraced and wreathed Agathon. At this point Agathon said: Undo Alcibiades' shoes, young man, so that he can recline at the table, as our third.

Yes, yes, said Alcibiades. But who is the third with us at the table? And at that he turned around and saw Socrates, and seeing him, jumped up and exclaimed: Oh Lord! What have

C we here? Is it Socrates? Lying in wait for me again? So, you're lying here—like you always do—suddenly appearing wherever I least expect you! Why have you come here now? And why are you lying here, and not beside Aristophanes or someone else who is a clown by choice? How do you contrive to be lying down beside the most beautiful man here?

And here Socrates interjected: Agathon—look! Will you help me? My love for this young man has become no trivial matter. From the very moment I fell in love with him it has

D ceased being possible for me either to look at or talk to a single good-looking person, but this fellow here becomes jealous of me and envious, and carries on fantastically, reviles me and just barely manages to keep his hands off me! Look —you see—I'm afraid he's going to carry on even now—please reconcile us—or protect me if he tries to be violent—I'm really completely terrified of this fellow's amorous rage!

No, said Alcibiades, there can be no reconciliation between you and me. But I'll take vengeance on you for these things later on. For now, Agathon, he went on, give me some of the fillets so that I can enwreathe this wonderful head here, and then he won't be able to accuse me of having made a garland for you, while he himself, the champion speaker of all—not only just the day before yesterday, like you, but always—I left uncrowned. And as he said this he took the fillets and made a garland for Socrates and then stretched out beside him. And when he had lain back, he spoke: Well, then, gentlemen—you look sober to me. This can't be allowed—you must drink! That's what you've agreed to, just now. So, I proclaim as Master of Revelry (until you've consumed enough) . . . myself! But look here, Agathon, have you got a great huge vessel? Oh, never mind, it's not necessary: Young man! Bring me that wine-cooler there!—he called out, seeing one that held more than a half-gallon. When he had seen to it that this was filled, he first drained it himself, then had it filled again for Socrates, and asserted at the same time: With Socrates, Gentlemen, my trick won't work. However much anyone asks him to drink, he drinks, and he's never the drunker for it. Then, when the boy had poured, Socrates drank.

And Eryximachus said: Is this the way we should behave, Alcibiades? Shouldn't we be saying anything over our cups, or singing? Should we simply gulp it down like sots?

And Alcibiades answered: Ah, Eryximachus, noblest son of a noble, sober sire!—Greetings!

And the same to you, responded Eryximachus. But how shall we do it?

Oh, let's do it the way you want. One must obey you,

For a single doctor's worth a parcel of others. . . .

So command us however you like.

All right then, listen, said Eryximachus. Before you arrived it had been agreed among us that each in turn, going
c   around to the right, would make as fine a speech as he could in praise of the god Love. And all the rest of us have spoken. But since you haven't spoken yet, and have been drinking, it's only just that you make a speech and when you've made your speech, to command Socrates to do whatever you want, and for him to do it to the one on his right, and so on for the others.

Ah, Eryximachus, answered Alcibiades, that sounds fine, but it isn't fair to compare a drunken man's oration with the speeches of sober men, and to expect them to be of equal
d   quality. Besides, my dear, hasn't Socrates convinced you of the things he said just now? Don't you know that everything is the opposite of what he has said? This one—whenever I praise anyone in his presence—a god or another man or whatever, he won't restrain himself from manhandling me!

Why don't you be still? said Socrates.

Oh, by Poseidon! exclaimed Alcibiades, Don't deny that! I won't praise a single other person in your presence.

Well, do it that way, then, urged Eryximachus, if you want. Praise Socrates.

What are you saying? asked Alcibiades. Do you think I should, Eryximachus? Shall I rush at the fellow and chastise him in front of you all?

e   Look here! cried Socrates, What are you planning? Are you going to praise me with ridicule? What are you going to do?

I shall tell the truth. Will you permit me?

Well, certainly, he said. I'll permit you—I order you—tell the truth!

I can't do it too soon, responded Alcibiades. But please do
215 this—if I say something that isn't true, catch me up right in the middle, if you wish, and say what it is that I'm falsifying. Because I won't falsify anything on purpose. But if I get

something I'm remembering mixed up, don't be surprised—
it's no easy matter for someone in my condition to give a
lucid and orderly account of your strangeness!

Alcibiades

To praise Socrates, gentlemen, I shall proceed as follows:
through similes. He will assume that I'm ridiculing him. But
the simile will be for the sake of the truth, not for ridicule.

B I assert he is most like the Sileni which sit in statuaries' shops
—the ones which the craftsmen carve to hold shepherd's pipes
or flutes, which, when they are opened into two, turn out
to have images of the gods inside. And I shall compare him,
too, with the satyr Marsyas.

  And you, yourself, Socrates, won't deny that you are like
these in looks. But you are like them in other respects besides
this—listen: you are an outrageous mocker, are you not?
do you deny it? If you don't agree, I can bring witnesses.

C And aren't you a flutist? A far more fabulous one than he.
His lips had the power to bewitch men, in those days, with
his instruments, but even now anyone who plays his music on
the flute can do the same. I mean, Olympus played the music
of Marsyas, his teacher; and whenever a good flutist, or even
a paltry flute girl plays his songs, all by themselves, because
the songs are divine they can inspire and reveal those who
belong to the gods and have received their mysteries. And
you are different from him only in that you do this same

D thing in speech, without instruments. Thus, when we hear
anyone else expressing his arguments—even a first rate rhet-
orician—practically no one gives it a second thought. But
when one hears you, or your discourses from someone else—
no matter how inept as a speaker—whether it's a woman who
hears it or a man or a schoolboy—we are all stupefied and
inspired. At least I, my friends, if I wouldn't show myself to

be hopelessly drunk, would take an oath on the degree to
which I myself have been affected by this man's words, and
E   still suffer now. When I hear him, I am worse than the
corybantes—these words of his make my heart throb and
tears come pouring out of my eyes; and I see a great many
others going through the same things. I've heard Pericles and
other good rhetoricians, and I've thought they spoke well;
but I never felt this sort of thing, my soul didn't thunder in
me, didn't rage at my slavish condition! But I have been
216   affected in this way many times by this Marsyas here, so that
it seemed to me that my own life was not worth living! And
you can't deny the truth of this, Socrates. Even now, I know
perfectly well that if I allowed myself to hear him again,
I'd have the same feelings—I wouldn't be able to resist. He
compels me to admit that while I am deficient in many respects I still neglect myself, and look to the affairs of Athens.
So I force my ears shut as against the Sirens, and run away, in
B   order not to grow old sitting there at his feet! But there is
one thing I have felt in his presence, alone among men, a
feeling which no one would have believed to be in me—shame
before someone. Before him alone I feel ashamed. For I
realize within myself that I am powerless to contradict him,
and that I ought to do what he commands, but that I turn
C   my back and submit to the honors of the masses. So I flee him,
sneaking off like a slave, and when I see him again I am
ashamed at the conclusions we came to. Many times I have
wished he would cease to exist among men! But if that happened I am sure that I would grieve even more—so that I
don't know what to do about the man!

So, these are the effects which the pipings of this Satyr
have had on me and many others. But now you'll really see
how much he and the creature I've compared him to are alike,
and how astonishing his nature really is. You may be sure
D   that not one of you knows him. However, I shall reveal him,
since I have already begun. For instance, you see that Socrates is sexually attracted to beautiful men, and is always

rapturously following them around? What is more that he is
ignorant of everything and knows nothing—that's the pose
he affects—now isn't this like the Silenus? Certainly it is. He
has donned this nature on the outside exactly like the carved
Silenus. But when the inner man is disclosed, would you
believe, fellow-drinkers, how much real sense* there is in
him? You should know that it doesn't matter at all to him
whether one is good-looking or not. Why, you couldn't believe to what extent he looks down on that sort of thing; or
whether one is wealthy, or has any other honor that may be
considered "happiness" by the crowd. He considers all that
sort of goods worth nothing, and we ourselves as nothing too
—I tell you—and he pretends to be ignorant, and spends his
whole life putting people on. I don't know if any one has seen
the images in this man when he is in earnest and has exposed
his inner self. I actually saw them once, and as a result, he
has seemed to me divine, all-golden, exquisite and miraculous.
And so, in brief, I must do whatever Socrates may demand
of me.

    Believing that he was really serious about my beauty, I
thought I had a godsend—a rare piece of luck. By gratifying
Socrates I would be able to hear all the things he knew—for I
really considered my looks a rare treasure. So, with this
intention—up to then I was not accustomed to meet him
without an attendant—I sent the attendant away and met him
alone. I must tell the whole truth before you; but pay close
attention, Socrates, and refute me if I distort a single fact! So
I met him, my friends, and we were entirely alone; I believed
that he would immediately begin to make love to me—and
I was happy. But—nothing of the sort happened. He talked
to me just the way he always did when we spent the day
together, and then he left me and went away! After this I

* The word Alcibiades uses here is σωφροσύνη. For a discussion of
the problems presented by this word see the note on its earlier
use in the dialogue, at 209B. (Translator's note.)

C   asked him to go to the gymnasium with me and I exercised with him, expecting to get what I wanted this way. So, he exercised with me, and wrestled with me quite often, when no one was around. And what is there to say? It got me nowhere!

Now, since I was accomplishing nothing with this sort of thing, I thought that I should attack the man head-on and not pull back, now that I had set myself to this seriously. I wanted to know, once and for all, what was going on. I in-
D   vited him to have dinner with me, you know, the way a lover does with plans for his darling. And this too he was reluctant to accept; however, in time I persuaded him. But the first time he came he wanted to leave as soon as he had eaten, and I felt too embarrassed not to let him go. But I made a plan for the next time. After we had eaten, I talked far into the night, and when he wanted to go, I pretended that it was too late, and forced him to stay. So he came to rest on the couch next to me, right where he had eaten, and no one else was sleeping in the room there with us.

E   Now, I could have told my story perfectly well before anyone up to this point. But from here on you wouldn't catch me telling it except that, while wine and children are truthful (as the saying goes: the wine works without the children!) and then, too, it would seem to me unjust to hide Socrates' magnificent disdain, when I was making a eulogy to him. And yet, I have the same feeling as the man who was
218 bitten by the snake. They say he didn't want to tell anyone what that experience was like unless they had been bitten themselves, since only such a person could understand and forgive him if he ran wild and raved in his agony. And you see I have been bitten by a more painful thing, and in the most painful way that one can be bitten—in the heart, or soul, or whatever else you call it—being stricken and bitten by the words of his philosophy, which hold on more cruelly than the adder in the soul of a young and not ungifted person, whenever they have grasped it, and make him do and say

B·A S K I N·

whatever they will! I see here Phaedrus, Agathon, Eryxima-
B   chus, Pausanias, Aristodemus, Aristophanes—there is no need
to mention Socrates himself—and others of the same sort.
All of you have had a share of the madness and ecstasy of
philosophy. So listen: you must forgive me for the things that
happened then, and for the things that are said now. But,
the servants and any one else who is ignorant and common—
put thick doors over your ears!

    So, my friends, when the light was extinguished and the
C   servants were outside, I thought that I ought not be cagey
with him, but rather it seemed right to speak freely about this
business. So, shaking him, I asked:

    Socrates—are you asleep?

    Not at all, he answered.

    Do you know what I think about all this?

    Why, what?

    I think, I announced, that you are my only worthy lover,
and yet you seem to hesitate even mentioning love to me.
And I feel this way: I would consider myself an utter fool
D   not to give you pleasure in this way—as well as in any other
way, if you had any need of my property or friends. I want
you to know that there is nothing more important to me than
becoming as virtuous as possible, and I think I can have no
better helper for this than you. Actually, I'd feel far more
shame before enlightened people if I didn't give my love to
a man like you, than I would before the know-nothings,
if I did!

    When he had heard what I had to say, he answered in that
extremely ironical way he always uses, very characteristically:

    My dear Alcibiades, you may not, in fact, be so foolish
E   after all, if what you are saying about me happens to be true
and there is some power in me through which you can get to
be a better man. You must perceive in me a sort of incredible
beauty, but of a kind, I mean, very different from your own
good looks. If you have observed this, and have decided to

try and have some share of it, that is, make a trade—beauty for beauty—well! You're trying to get for yourself the real thing in beauty, in place of the sham. That's really the old "gold-for-bronze" exchange! But, my happy friend, look sharp, I may fool you, and turn out not to be what you take me for. The vision of the intellect begins to be acute when that of the eye is starting to weaken, and you're far from that, as yet!

When I heard this I said: There is absolutely no difference between the way I feel about things and what I've said. But you yourself must decide what would be best for both of us.

Ah, he said, well put; in the days to come we'll work out these and other matters, and do what seems to us the best thing.

So then, when I heard him say this, and thinking that I'd shot my own words into him like darts and had got to him with what I'd said, I stood, and without letting him say another word wrapped my own gown around him—it was winter, you know. I lay down under his worn cloak, put my arms around him—around this daemonic and truly marvellous man—and stayed by him for the whole night. (And Socrates, you can't say that I'm making up any of this story!) But despite my having done all this, he proved so superior and showed such contempt and laughed me so to scorn for my youth, that he insulted the one thing I really thought was worth anything, Gentlemen of the Jury—for you must be the judges of Socrates' arrogance—realize, then, that when I got up—I swear by every god and goddess—after having slept with Socrates, it had been in no way different from having slept with a father or elder brother!

Now what sort of mood do you imagine I was in after this affair? First of all I considered myself rejected, but then I got to wondering at his nature—his intelligence and manliness. I had come on a man of such wisdom and strength that I would not have believed I could have found him! Whereas I was unable to deprive myself of his company, I was also

thoroughly unsuccessful at seducing him. I came to realize
that he was far more invulnerable in every way to bribery
than Ajax had been to the sword, and in the only area where
I had believed he could be overcome, he eluded me! I was
really at a loss! I wandered around, enslaved by this man as
no one ever was by anyone!

All of this happened to me, you realize, and then, later,
there was that campaign that we were both on to Potidaea.
There we were mess-mates. Now first of all, not only did he
surpass me in his ability to tolerate hardship, but everyone
else too! Whenever we were forced to go without food be-
220 cause we were cut off (which often happens on a campaign),
everybody else completely lacked endurance. Then, again,
when there was plenty, he was the only man who was fully
capable of appreciating it. And furthermore, although he
didn't want to drink, whenever he was forced into it he beat
everybody, and what is most remarkable of all, no man has
ever seen Socrates drunk! My guess is that the proof of this is
going to be apparent pretty soon.

And then there were his powers of endurance in winter—
B and the winters there are terrible. He performed other mir-
acles: once, when there was an amazingly hard frost, and
there was either no going out at all, or else if you did have to
go out, you got all dressed to do so by putting on overshoes
and then wrapping up the feet in felts and sheepskins. Well,
this man went out into that weather with a cloak on, exactly
like what he usually wore, and went about on the ice in
bare feet, more easily than the other men with their overshoes! The soldiers suspected him of looking down on them.

C So that's that. But this thing, too, the great man dared and
did while we were on that expedition, and it is well worth
hearing. He thought of something, and right there on the
spot, from dawn on, he stood fixed, contemplating whatever
it was. For as long as the solution didn't come to him, he
didn't move; he stuck to his search. It got to be midday, and
the men watched this going on and marvelled at him, and

told one another about how Socrates had stood there thinking about something since early morning. At last, a group of
D   Ionians, when it had got to be evening, ate, and because it was summer, carried their bedrolls outside, both to sleep where it was cool, and at the same time to keep an eye on him and see if he'd stand there all night too. And he did stand there, until it got to be dawn, and the sun came up. Then he went away, first turning and making a prayer to the sun.

And if you want, there was the fighting. It's quite proper to describe him in this respect, since it was in that battle for
E   which the high commanders gave me the citation that he, of all my men, saved my life! He refused to desert me when I was wounded, and he saved me and my armor too. And Socrates, I did right then and there demand that the commanders dedicate the citation to you, so you shouldn't blame me for what happened, and you can't say I'm lying. But when the generals wanted to give the medal to me just because of my position, you yourself were even more eager than they for me to have it.

221   And what's more, my friends, it was worth anything to see Socrates when the army was making its retreat, fleeing from Delios. I happened to be present, on horseback, while he was bearing arms. The men were all scattered, and he was making his retreat along with Laches. So I happened along, and seeing him, I shouted at them right away to be brave, and promised I wouldn't leave the two of them. And here I saw Socrates behave even more beautifully than he had at Potidaea. I myself had less to fear, since I was on horseback. First of all, he was much better at keeping cool than Laches. Then
B   I noticed that he marched along exactly the way he does here at home, as you've described it, Aristophanes, with *strutting and tossing of sidelong looks*, slowly looking around at everybody—friend or enemy—making it obvious to all from any distance, that if anybody tried to touch this man,

he'd put up one hell of a wild fight! And that was how he
and his comrade got away safely. When people act this way
C   in battle no one bothers them; they chase after those who run
away helter-skelter.

Now there are many other fabulous things that one might
say in praise of Socrates. But while as much could probably
be said for his other characteristics, one could probably say
them about someone else, and it's his difference from other
men, whether ancient or modern, which is his most amazing
trait! For what Achilles was like, one could draw a com-
D   parison with Brasidas, or others, and then, again, for Pericles,
there is Nestor, and Antenor, and others I could mention.
And all other great men can be likened to someone; but this
man's nature is so peculiar, both in himself and in the things
he says, that one could search and never find his like, not
among anyone living today, nor among the ancients, unless it
is among the ones I say one has to compare him with—no
man, certainly, but those Sileni and Satyrs.

Oh—I neglected that at the beginning—the fact that his
E   words remind one very much of the Sileni that get opened
up. When you listen to what Socrates says, at first it sounds
ridiculous. His arguments are all clothed by words and
phrases which are like the hide of an impudent Satyr, for he
speaks of millstones and pack-asses, of smithies, shoemaker's
shops and tanners, and through all these things seems to be
repeating himself over and over, so that any ignorant fool
222   would laugh at the things he says. But if one sees them opened
up and penetrates into them, one finds to begin with that
they are the only discourses that make any sense; and later
that they have a great divinity, that they are filled with the
images of virtue, in themselves, and when they are extended
to their fullest meaning they encompass everything that
it becomes a man to contemplate who is seeking to achieve
the beautiful and the good.

That, my friends, is how I choose to praise Socrates. I have found fault with him too, and have mixed into my account

B   to you the things he did to enrage me. I know perfectly well that it's not only to me that he's done these things. There was Charmides, Glaucon's son, and Euthydemus, the son of Diocles, and a whole lot of others, as well, whom this "lover" utterly deceived, getting them to woo him, so that he was more their darling than their lover! I'm addressing myself particularly to you, Agathon, so that you'll not be tricked by him. Since you're being forewarned, you can escape the things we went through, and not be a fool who, as the saying goes, has to learn from his own mistakes.

C   When Alcibiades had said all this there was some laughter at his candor, because he seemed to be still in love with Socrates. At this point Socrates spoke up.

You seem quite sober to me, Alcibiades. Otherwise you would never have tried to hide your reason for saying all these things with that elaborate roundabout of circumlocution, and then attach it to the conclusion of your speech like an afterthought. As if you weren't saying the whole thing

D   for the sake of setting Agathon and me at odds! You imagine that I have to love you and nobody else, while Agathon has to be loved by no one but you! But you haven't fooled me. That Satyric and Silenus piece of yours was really transparent. Look, dear Agathon, don't let him get away with it. Be prepared, so that he won't split us up.

E   Then Agathon said, Well, Socrates, what you're saying is probably true. And I take his sitting between you and me to be aimed at separating us from one another. He's not going to succeed, though; if I want to be there beside you, I will.

Certainly, said Socrates, sit down here, beyond me.

My god! said Alcibiades. What I have to go through with this man! He thinks he has to do me one better every time! But at least, you amazing fellow, you should let Agathon sit between us.

But that's impossible! Socrates said. You've just made a

speech in praise of me, and I've got to praise the one on my right. So, if Agathon sits beyond you—won't he have to praise me, again, before he gets praised instead by me? But

222 please! my sweet madman, don't begrudge my praising this boy. I really do want to extol him, with all my heart!

Ah-hah! exclaimed Agathon. Alcibiades, there's not a chance that I'd stay where I am! By all means, I'd rather be a migrant, if I can get Socrates to praise me!

That's the way things go, Alcibiades said. It's always the same. When Socrates is around it's impossible for anyone else to have anything to do with the beauties. Notice how ingeniously he found the right argument to persuade this one here to sit beside him!

B So Agathon got up and sat beside Socrates. Suddenly there were a lot of revelers at the doors, and finding them open (for someone was just leaving), they marched straight in and joined the people. The place was filled with utter confusion, there wasn't the slightest semblance of order anymore, and they were compelled to consume vast quantities of wine.

C Here Aristodemus says that he believes Eryximachus and Phaedrus and some others left, and he himself fell asleep and slept for a long time, it having been the season of long nights, but toward morning, when the cocks were already crowing, he was awakened. When he'd awakened, he saw the others sleeping or gone away, while only Agathon, Aristophanes, and Socrates were left awake and drinking from a great vessel, passing it around from left to right. Socrates was talking to them. Aristodemus says that he can't remember the

D rest of what was being said (since he'd not been awake for the beginning and was sleepy), but in the main he says that Socrates was forcing them to agree that it was possible for the same man to know how to write comedy and tragedy, and that the skilled tragedian can write comedy as well. Well, they were being forced to agree to all this, but they

weren't following it very actively, and were dozing off. Aristophanes dropped off first, and by the time it was fully daylight, Agathon had too. Socrates, when he had seen the two of them off to sleep, got up and went away, and Aristodemus followed, just as always.

When he reached the Lyceum he bathed, and spent the rest of the day just as any other, and when the day was spent that way, and it got to be evening, he went home to rest.

The Nature of Love

Philosophers who have written on love—and as Plato noticed in his day, they are very few—have mainly discussed four issues: (1) the objects of love, and whether loved objects are one sort of thing or diverse; (2) the sort of state love is—whether it is a sensation or feeling, an attitude, an emotion, a belief, a desire, or some combination of these; (3) the relation between love and desire (which may, or may not, be answered under the previous topic); and (4) the relation between love and valuation. I shall briefly discuss the first three of these issues, but my main concern shall be the last.

The question concerning the objects of love is actually several issues which are sometimes confused. Many thinkers have held that there is one proper sort of love object which is not, however, always or exclusively loved by everyone. Such thinkers have to allow that what people actually love, and what they would love if they were moral or prudent, may be different. In this category I would place Plato and Freud. Both hold that we can be mistaken in our love objects, and experience great frustration and despair because of such mistakes. Another distinction must be made. There are thinkers who would insist that, though we may actually love an object that is not worthy of love, we could not love the object unless we *believed* it was worthy of love. Plato, again, is an instance of this position. Freud and certain Christian philosophers, for example St. Augustine, are instances of thinkers who hold, on the contrary, that there is a certain sort of object which is worthy of love, and that people may mistakenly love things not of that sort, *and* that they need *not* think what they love to be of that sort.

The things people actually love and, Plato notwithstanding, what people think worthy of love, are as various—indeed more various—than one can imagine. Whether there is one *proper* sort of object of love, for example, sexually gratifying objects (Freud), God (St. Augustine), good things (Plato), pleasant things (Mill), happiness-giving things (I would say), is a question I cannot discuss. Though this is one central issue for a complete theory of love, it overshadows it entirely. Indeed one reason that so few philosophers write about love is that what people *actually* love cannot be determined philosophically without grotesque oversimplification; and the *proper* object of love is considered in a division of philosophy all its own: ethics and value-theory.

All writers on love have agreed that loving something necessarily implies valuing it. Perhaps we can best see the sort of psychological state love is if we begin with this. Love, then, can be thought of as a form of valuation. Clearly many valuations do not involve love: I value my car and I do not love it. Is there a form of valuation such that we can say, when someone values something in that way, they love that object? The concept of intrinsic value is immediately suggested. Can we hold that people love that which they value intrinsically, that is, what they value in and of itself;[1] and conversely, that whatever they love, they value for its own sake?

An objection to this is that love involves emotional attachment, or affection, and that many cases of intrinsic valuation do not. This is especially clear (the objection goes) when the object of my valuation is general, for instance, the welfare of mankind. In such a case, surely, it makes no sense to speak of emotional attachment, hence there is no love.

My reply is that there is more than one sort of love, and that

---

1. I shall not try to define the concept of intrinsic value, but shall assume it to be sufficiently clear for my discussion of love. Roughly, I mean by intrinsic value, the property an object has of being worthy of choice independently of its consequences for other experiences of the agent or other persons; and by intrinsic disvalue, the property of being worthy of avoidance independently of the object's consequences for other experiences of the agent or other persons. Plato makes this distinction in *Republic* II (357B). The opposite of intrinsic value is ordinarily called 'instrumental value.'

many kinds of love (at least relations we now call 'love') cannot conceivably involve emotional attachment. Thus, I would say, the objection which is brought against some forms of intrinsic valuation being love applies equally to some forms of love; and this shows that the objection fails to understand the connection between love and emotion and feeling.

I assume that a basic distinction in love is according to whether its object is individual or general. In the former case there is an emotional attachment, of one person to another thing (person or nonperson), in the latter there is not. For distinctions' sake let us say that in the former case there is a presupposition of affection. This concept is vague and broad—enough to stretch from the love of inanimate things, and animals, to those friendships which are serious enough to involve love, through the feelings of parent and child, through the most emotional, sexual, relationships, and at an opposite extreme, to sexual relationships which are comparatively free of other interest or involvement.

In all of these cases, I suggest, besides intrinsic valuation there is the direction of feeling upon an individual. We can roughly characterize the kinds of love by the kinds of feelings and emotions and their intensity and duration, yet the distinctions are very rough and unclear, so much so that people often cannot compare and distinguish their own relationships. Nor can we single out one feeling or emotion which alone constitutes a type of love relationship: any feeling or emotion, *under the appropriate circumstances*, may be expressive of love *or* the absence of love. It is the *pattern* of feeling and behavior, in their circumstances, which tells us whether love exists and what sort, in ourselves or in others. And the possible patterns are infinitely various and complicated. Thus we cannot define the kinds of love which fall within this broad class, nor can we define the class itself beyond saying that it requires positive intrinsic valuation and positive emotional attachment directed toward an individual. In practice, when we require more specific or exact distinctions, we usually classify our relationships by their *objects* rather than by sorting and describing our feelings.

Yet we also recognize a form of love which is more generalized: the love of mankind, of animals or kinds of animals, of kinds of activities (chess, skiing), of kinds of things (flowers, the sea). In these cases the attitude manifests itself largely in the willingness and cheerfulness with which we engage in certain kinds of behavior, and by our preferences—the things we choose to do, to concern ourselves with, to nurture, as opposed to those which we ignore, neglect, or forget. We find ourselves pleasantly occupied with these things, and feel a sense of loss when we are kept from being engaged with them for great lengths of time. Some might question the term 'love' as applied to such things. Can we find anything importantly similar between the love of gardening and the love of humanity, and between both of these and the love of a man for his wife? I am not ashamed to see, even in such different cases, one centrally important feature: high intrinsic value placed upon an element of one's life. To this extent, the common use of the term 'love,' to cover such diverse cases, seems entirely justified.

Of course when the object of love is general, a *kind* of thing, the quality and intensity of feeling or emotion is very different. But even for these cases, feeling cannot be completely absent. For example, consider a philanthropist (literally, a lover of mankind) who shows by acts of generosity that he values the well-being of others intrinsically. (For instance, he uses his money to alleviate suffering.) Such a man may not have feelings of tenderness or affection toward those he assists, nor any emotion whatever. Much less will he long to be with them, to live with them, or have sexual feelings about them. Thus according to the first conception of love he would not be said to love them. Even so people must be able to act upon his feelings. One who feels nothing when he sees a picture of a starving child, or reads about the suffering of needy people, should not be counted a lover of mankind. Those who lack feelings in such circumstances, and still act in ways which promote the welfare of the suffering, may do so out of a sense of duty or in order to *appear* concerned. They may be *benefactors* of mankind. But they are not, I believe, *lovers* of mankind even in the most abstract sense, nor do they consider the benefits they confer to be intrinsically worthwhile. Their concern is with the imperatives of duty or custom, or the benefits philanthropy brings to *them*.

This suggests there is more in common between the two kinds of love—love of individual, as opposed to general, objects—than one might expect, for both require feelings of some sort, under some circumstances, as a condition of love. Further, we cannot define conditions which decisively test the presence or absence of either sort of love. In both cases a very wide variety of feelings, in all sorts of different circumstances, may be relevant as indications of its presence or absence. The mistakes people make by giving undue importance to one sort of feeling, in one sort of circumstance, are, of course, notorious!

I shall assume, then, that love must contain a valuational and emotional element, and since both of these admit of great difference of kind and of degree, love too may vary greatly in the value it places on its object, and the feelings it has about it, both in kind and in degree. And I shall assume that people love that which they value intrinsically, and that whatever they love, they value intrinsically. These assumptions are controversial, but I have gone as far as I can in this context to indicate my reasons for them.

A major disagreement among writers on love and the topic I want mainly to discuss, concerns the *relation* of valuation and love. When we love something we value it intrinsically: do we love it *because* we value it, or do we value it *because* we love it? In the former case we must believe the object of our love to have certain value properties, as a precondition of loving it. In the latter case our love is a precondition of the objects' having value to us.

Christian *agape* is a concept of the latter sort. It is held that God's love for man is not *due* to the value of man, God does not love man *because* of a value possessed by human beings; rather, the love of God is bestowed as a gift, and human beings have value through this bestowal. Also, though man's love for God cannot be thought of in this way, men may love one another with *agape*: "Freely give, as freely ye have received." It is also held that this sort of love is higher: it is *better* to love without a reason, than with a reason. It is also held that one cannot love another person *as a person* unless one loves unconditionally, or for no reason, and thus with *agape*.[2]

Platonic *eros*, on the contrary, is the concept of love as motivated by the belief that the object of love is good or beautiful or valuable in some other way.[3]

I want first to discuss certain fallacious criticisms of the Platonic view. Then I will try to formulate considerations which will allow us to settle the dispute between the two theories.

2. The most influential work, advancing a distinction between *agape* and *eros*, is the three-volume study by Anders Nygren, *Agape and Eros*, first published in 1929; references and quotations in this article are all to the latest English translation, by Philip S. Watson (Philadelphia: The Westminster Press, 1953). The study is the starting point of the studies of Denis De Rougemont, *Love and the Western World*, trans. by Montgomery Belgian (New York: Harcourt, Brace and Co., 1940), and M. C. D'Arcy, *The Mind and Heart of Love* (London: Faber, 1945), and gives important background for two other worthwhile studies, *The Nature of Love: Plato to Luther* by Irving Singer (New York: Random House, 1966), and *Platonic Love* by Thomas Gould (New York: The Free Press, 1963). I have no space to discuss these works here in detail, though I will attempt to correct certain misunderstandings of Plato which are current in some of them. Nygren's conception of *agape*, as opposed to *eros*, is stated by him in the following terms: (1) "Agape is spontaneous and 'unmotivated'" (p. 75); (2) "Agape is 'indifferent to value'" (p. 77); (3) "Agape is creative" (p. 78), that is *agape* creates value in the object of love; (4) "Agape is the initiator of fellowship with God" (p. 80), that is, *agape* is the basis of the relationship of man and God. In contrast, according to Nygren, (1) "Eros is the 'love of desire,' or acquisitive love"; (2) "Eros is man's way to the divine—as opposed to God's approach to man—(3) "Eros is egocentric love" (p. 175).

3. Platonic *eros*, in one sense, involves a great deal besides: Plato's views on knowledge, reason, and desire; his dualism of being and becoming; his claim that the form of the Good is the highest object of love. I shall not be concerned here with this, but only one part of his theory, and a part which many would accept who disagree with him on other matters: that a belief in the value (the goodness, beauty, or other) of the object of love, is a precondition of love. The traditional Christian philosophy is Platonistic on many of these other points. I am concerned here only with the contrast between *eros* and *agape*.

In the literature on love one often sees arguments against Platonic love of this sort:

1) All *eros*-love is acquisitive/egocentric/nonpersonal;
2) There is a very important sort of love which is not acquisitive/egocentric/nonpersonal; therefore,
3) There is a very important sort of love which is not *eros*.

I shall show that Platonic love is quite capable of being nonacquisitive, nonegocentric, and personal, thus that the first premise of this argument is false. There is no such simple way of deciding between *eros* and *agape*.

One criticism of *eros* is that since *eros* is desire, or at least cannot exist without desire,[4] it is acquisitive, in a sense intended to be incompatible with the selfless, bestowal characteristics of *agape*. For instance, Nygren writes:

> even where Eros seems to be a desire to give it is still in the last resort a "Will-to-possess"; for Plato was fundamentally unaware of any other form of love than acquisitive love. *Agape and Eros*, p. 176)

And in his book *The Nature of Love*, Irving Singer says:

> For desire is always acquisitive, and its object a mere com-

4. The latter, and not the former, is actually Plato's stated position in the *Symposium:* Love, he says, desires its object (200A). He does not say that love is a desire, much less that love and desire are the same. That Love desires its object means, in nonfigurative language, that whoever loves something, desires that which they love. The strongest interpretation, which I do not believe can be justifiably attributed to Plato, is that whoever desires something, loves that which they desire. It should also be noted, in interpreting Plato, that his claim that there is no love without desire does not imply (a) that love is *nothing but* desire, nor (b) that love is directed to what we do not have or possess. For Plato specifically points out that we can desire what we have; for this means that we desire to continue to have it. Thus assuming that people desire to continue to have what they love, we will not find any cases in which people have and love something, but contrary to Plato's theory, do *not* desire it.

modity designed to satisfy. As Platonic eros is the organism striving to overcome deficiencies, so too is desire an attempt to eliminate a state of need or want . . . as an interest in the object itself, one that refuses to treat the object as merely a means to satisfaction, love is not reducible to *any* desire. (p. 89)

These writers can only make the charges they do by ignoring a very large class of desires. Desire is not acquisitive in those cases in which the object of my desire is the welfare, happiness, or satisfaction of some other person or group of people. Nor is it incompatible with my having an interest in the object itself, in such cases as when I desire and take satisfaction in another's happiness for his sake (and *not* because his achieving happiness allows me to realize my desire for his happiness!).

A similar mistake is made in the charge that *eros* is egocentric. Since *eros*-love is founded on the value of the love-object, it is assumed to follow that the lover seeks to aggrandize himself through his love. To quote Nygren again:

But the clearest proof of the egocentric nature of Eros is its intimate connection with *eudaimonia*. The aim of love is to gain possession of an object which is regarded as valuable and which man feels he needs. . . . Plato is especially concerned to emphasize this point. "It is by the acquisition of good things," he says, "that the happy are made happy." . . . To love the good, therefore, is the same as to desire to possess the good and to possess it *permanently* . . . but in this desire, too, the egocentric will is in evidence. (p. 180)

Nygren also writes:

all desire, or appetite, and longing, is more or less egocentric. (p. 180)

To call all desires "egocentric" is to deprive the term of all (but its pejorative) meaning. What matters is the *object* of the desire. Desires differ as their objects differ. My desire for a drink is egocentric, since it concerns *my* having a drink. My desires for the betterment of mankind, an end of poverty, a permanent peace, and so on, concern myself indirectly or not at all. It is sophistry to say that my interest in these matters derives from an interest in my own welfare. What if it does? I still have a genuine interest in them, in my present state: they are what I desire, and my desire is satisfied by virtue of someone else attaining something valuable to them. An egocentric man rates the satisfactions of other people lower than his own; it is in his system of values and the accompanying desires that he is egocentric. All men are alike in trying to satisfy their desires, and thus it shows nothing about the egocentricity of a concept of love to show that it involves desire. According to Plato men desire beauty and goodness everywhere: in the world of change they seek to create it as artists and statesmen; as educators they create it in other souls and themselves; they admire and contemplate it in the unchanging world of forms. In this they find happiness. But there is no reason to conclude that they view this beauty and goodness simply as means to their happiness or satisfaction.[5] For people do find satisfaction in contemplating that which they consider desirable for its own sake.

Platonic *eros* is often criticized as being incompatible with the love of persons. The assumption behind this criticism is a general principle of this form: if a person loves x because he believes x to have the property G, he must be using x as a means to acquiring G.

Take, for initial consideration, an ordinary, nonemotional sort of instance. I love a certain wine; I love it *because of* its taste, aroma, and color. Does it follow that I use the wine as a means to enjoying its taste, aroma, and color? Not at all. The idea of means

---

5. In the *Republic* Socrates says that the best things are those which are desirable both for their consequences and in themselves. And he argues that people who attain these things without their (normal) consesequences, are happier than people who attain their (normal) consequences without the things themselves. Thus Plato rates as the happiest existence that in which the self contemplates things, valuable in themselves, without reference to their consequences. Thus clearly he does not think that we find them valuable *because of* their consequences.

and end, so used, is completely inappropriate. If I desire something only as a means, I care about it only because it may be used to cause something else which I love per se. My loving a wine because it has certain properties, could mean that I love the properties per se and the wine only because it brings me that which I love. Yet it has a more natural interpretation: the properties are what it is *about* the wine, which is the basis of my love for *it*. On the first interpretation, we are asked to suppose that people love properties, and objects only as means, whenever their love has a reason. It is more plausible, I suggest, that when people love for a reason, they love objects, but conditionally upon believing that their reason is satisfied. When I say that I love x because it is G, I am giving an *explanation* of my love for x by the reference to G. I am saying, in effect, that I am moved to love anything which is G, insofar as it is G; and since x is a G, I love x. Notice that in the conclusion the object of my love is x, not the property G (my reason for loving x).

Thus it does not follow from Plato's claim that we love persons (or anything else) because we believe them to be beautiful and good, that we really love the properties of beauty and goodness per se, and do not really love persons per se. In making this statement he is arguing that our love follows a general pattern: it occurs only where we believe something to be good, and it is the stronger where we believe greater good to be present. Now it is certainly true that Plato believed that we loved the Good and the Beautiful more than anything else, and that other things are loved because they resemble the Good and the Beautiful. Yet the Good and the Beautiful are themselves good and beautiful things loved *because of* their goodness and beauty. Also, they are loved more than other things only because they are held to be more beautiful than other things. Further, the relation of lower things to the Good and the Beautiful is not the relation of thing to property, but of imitation to reality, copy to exemplar.

This mistake is difficult to stamp out. We are familiar with the perennial but not very bright complaint: you don't love *me*, you just love my G (for 'G' may be substituted 'money,' 'body,' 'brains,' and so forth). The basis of the unhappiness expressed by this remark, however, is being loved for the *wrong* qualities, not the wish for the lover to be indifferent to *all* the beloved's qualities! In the case of Plato the plausibility of this mistaken principle has a different source. We think the love of persons is the highest form of love, and we feel that Plato is deeply wrong when he says that (1) other people are loved because of a resemblance they bear to the Good and (2) the Good is more valuable, and more satisfying to love, than persons. And Plato is wrong in these two points. Yet it is not a consequence of this system of values, that there can be no genuine love of persons per se.[6] Plato's hierarchy is not a hierarchy of merely instrumental goods leading to the Good; it is a hierarchy of intrinsic goods. Each member of the hierarchy is less good, hence less worthy of love, than any member above it; and each depends on the highest good for what goodness and beauty it has. Yet since each is beautiful and satisfying (in its limited, imperfect way), each is (in its limited, imperfect way) intrinsically good.

The conclusion to be drawn from these arguments is that *eros* is not distinguishable from *agape* by being egocentric, acquisitive, or nonpersonal. If they are correct I believe there is no possibility of singling out cases which are definitely examples of *agape* but not of *eros* by the sort of interest involved. For both *eros* and *agape* are valuational. And we cannot point to cases of nonacquisitive, nonegocentric, personal love and say: that is *agape*, not *eros*. It is usually assumed that the reverse is possible: we can distinguish cases of *eros* from *agape*, as, for instance, where sexual love occurs completely divorced from other interests in the partner. Yet this assumption is merely another form of the first mistake just discussed: it is simply prejudice that sexual love must be exploitative, or use

6. Singer claims that it is: "Plato emphasizes that love for another person is primarily a desire for the goodness which is in him. In other words, it is not the other person as a person that the Platonic lover cares about. He loves his beloved, not in himself, but only for the sake of goodness or beauty. The Platonic lover does not love anyone: he loves only the Good" (*The Nature of Love*, p. 87).

its object as a means to selfish enjoyment. Sexual love can be as spontaneous and unmotivated as *agape* traditionally conceived; it too can creatively bestow value on its object. The essential feature of *agape* is its being a love which does not follow criteria but creates them in the love itself. This may be a feature of pure sexuality as much as in the less physically directed forms of love. But where sexual love is exploitative, where it uses the object simply as a means of satisfaction, there is no *eros* present and indeed, no love properly so-called; for it was laid down earlier in this paper that all love views its object as valuable for its own sake and not merely as a means.

These moral considerations show no distinction between *agape* and *eros*. Either sort of love is as capable of dignifying its object as the other. Nor should this surprise us, after all, when we consider that we did not distinguish the two by a moral criterion. We have said that we must decide whether love creates a valuation (*agape*) or proceeds from one (*eros*), not whether love uses a certain sort of valuative criterion for its objects (thereby including some sorts of thing and excluding others). Our concern is with the relation between love and valuation generally.

We may make a fresh approach by considering a classic text for this issue, the discussion in Plato's *Euthyphro*. In this dialogue Euthyphro has defined Piety as that which all of the gods love (7A); Impiety as that which all of the gods hate (9E). Further Socrates and Euthyphro agree that the gods love the Holy because it is holy—they agree that it is *not* holy *because* it is loved (10C). Socrates then points out a fault in the definition:

> It seems, Euthyphro, when you were asked to say what Piety is, you did not wish to make plain its nature and told instead something which has been done to it, namely that it pertains to Piety to be loved by all of the gods. But you did not say what its *being* is. Do not hide it from me, if you please, but starting again from the beginning tell me what Piety is, and never mind whether it is loved by the gods, or anything else has happened to it. (11A–B)

Socrates' distinction between what Piety really is, and what belongs to it by virtue of an act of approval or love, may give one key to the difference between Plato and St. Paul. For to Plato it is incidental to the pious, something which merely pertains to it, that the gods love it. And this presupposes that the value characteristics of things are independent of the approval or disapproval of the gods, that the gods approve that which they *find* to be worthy of their approval. For Plato, then, value characteristics exist *prior* to the beliefs of either gods or men.

To Plato the creative activities of men and god presuppose an ideal or model which guides the act of creation. One of the highest forms of creative activity in men is legislation, but the man-created laws and rules which guide life are not basic value principles but "recipes" by which men may be guided in patterning themselves after the higher realities. The human statesman gazes at the ideals of Justice, Wisdom, and Courage, and like a painter forms his creation, the human state, in their likeness (*Republic* 500C–501A). And when Plato describes the creation of the world he speaks of god as contemplating and copying in as much detail as possible an uncreated model of the world (*Timaeus* 30C–D). To Plato thought is always and essentially directed to externally existing objects (*Parmenides* 132B–C, *Republic* 478B). And action and feeling, in their highest form, are guided by thought.

Christian thought takes a major initiative in its doctrine of creation, according to which God not only makes the world out of nothing, but in his act of creation gives the standards by which the world and everything in it are to be judged. The love of the Christian god, according to Nygren (and in Paul's epistles and the parables of Jesus) is not measured out in terms of some antecedently given scale of values. The values of things, in relation to God, are dependent, in this sense: the love of God creates the intrinsic value which belongs to the objects of his creation. It is not something which merely pertains to good things, that they should be loved by God. Being good and being God-loved, are essentially the same. Of course for men in this interpretation, the value characteristics are prior—exist independently of *their* beliefs and attitudes. For this reason it might be thought that human love could not confer value on its object in the same manner as the divine, hence could not be *agape*.[7]

Here is a difference between the Platonic and Christian points of view which may elucidate the difference between *eros* and *agape*. Can we say that philosophers who accept the *eros* view of love do so *because* they believe value properties to exist independently of the attitudes and beliefs of persons (divine and human)? And that philosophers who believe that values are relative are inclined for that reason, to accept the concept of *agape* over that of *eros?* This, I believe, is the basic difference in the two concepts of love. If so then the issue of whether *eros* or *agape* is the correct conception of love reduces to the question of whether values are objective or relative (either to man or to the will of God).

However, there is a way of construing the emphasis on *eros* rather than *agape* which does not assume objective values. Rather, this second way assumes the primacy of value *beliefs* over *feelings*. For one element in the concept of *eros* is that the *beliefs* the lover has in the value of the object cause his love for the object. Thus while earlier we stated that *eros* involved a prior recognition that its object is intrinsically valuable, we may now define it solely by reference to the lover's beliefs. So defined the concept of *eros* no longer carries a presupposition of the objectivity of values. By contrast, *agape*, on this model, would be a love in which the (spontaneous, unreasoned) feeling of the lover for the object causes him to believe the object has intrinsic value. The controversy then centers around whether value-beliefs and reasons cause love-feelings, or conversely, whether love-feelings cause value-beliefs.[8]

7. Nygren claims as much, for instance, *Agape and Eros*, p. 125.
8. We may take two views of this characterization of *eros*. Either we may suppose the lover believes the value of his love-object is objective or not. If the former, then the lover believes (1) that the object of his love is intrinsically valuable, (2) that it has this value objectively, and (3) these beliefs cause him to love this object. If the latter, then we leave out condition (2). In the former alternative our concept of *eros* no longer commits us to the existence of objective intrinsic values, but

It seems to me that if we redefine the issue between *eros* and *agape* as we have done, *neither* concept is by itself sufficient to explain all cases of love. Rather, some lovers and loves will be cases of *eros* and some of *agape*. An important difference exists between those who let their emotions be guided by their beliefs and whose love thus has an ethical or prudential cast, and those whose love is unmotivated by reasons. Though both sorts of person will value the object of their love intrinsically, a very important difference obtains in their *reasons* for ascribing value to the object of love. On the one hand, the beloved is thought to be valuable because certain value-making conditions are thought to be fulfilled, for example, it is intelligent or beautiful. In the second case, the value-making condition is the love itself, which does not in turn exist for a reason that the lover can offer. Since no value-making condition exists or at least is operative as a belief of the lover, it is proper to say that the love itself creates the value belief.

I think that both have existed and hence that both are possible. The question which remains is whether one sort is preferable, and hence whether we should cultivate one form—at least in some circumstances—in preference to the other. The answer is clearly that an unqualified preference for either sort would be wrong. No general answer is possible since the causes of love, whether feelings or beliefs, *may* be either destructive or constructive in their effects.

---

only to the belief in their existence. In this case, if the belief is false or unprovable, *eros* would involve a kind of illusion not unlike the sort of illusion Kant felt existed in our inescapable belief in an external, intelligible world. In the second alternative we are no longer committed even to this illusion. To make this clearer consider the ethics of Jean-Paul Sartre. He holds that each man creates his own system of moral rules and correlated values, hence he denies the objective status of values. Yet within each man's system, so viewed, a distinction between intrinsic and nonintrinsic values may be made. *Agape* may be similarly defined in two ways. Either one may maintain that the lover has a love-feeling for an object which causes him (1) to believe the object is intrinsically valuable and (2) to believe this value is objective, or one may hold that the love-feeling simply causes the value-belief as in (1) with the omission of the condition stated in (2).

A person who bases his love on reasons may take as his reasons a selfish and short-term consideration, or a false assessment of the character of the beloved; and a love founded on "pure" emotion may be morbid or temporary or exploitative. In other cases important values may attach to a spontaneous, unmotivated love, or to the rational assessment of its object prior to a full emotional commitment. There is no empirical warrant for say.ing that human love must follow either course if it is to be "true love," and no basis for holding up either form as the highest since excesses are possible in the direction of rationalization or feeling.

In summary: My concern has been to survey the question of love as it now exists for us, to bring out the issues involved in it, and suggest answers to some of these issues. One issue is the nature of the object of love. I am much more cautious than Plato (and many other earlier writers) in attempting to give a general characterization of the actual objects or motives of human love. It is possible, I think, to achieve a theory of the proper objects of human love, but it is not possible to circumscribe human love within the limits of propriety! A second issue is a general description of the sort of psychological state love is. I suggested that love is not to be identified with any emotion or feeling, but rather with valuation. I hold that love is the same as intrinsic valuation, and that its relation to emotion and feeling (1) varies immensely according to the *sort* of love we are concerned with, and (2) is such a complex relationship, so dependent upon circumstances, that neither love in general nor any particular sort of love can be defined by the pattern of feelings involved in it. A third issue is the relation of love to desire. Here, I believe, Plato is entirely right: there is no love without desire for the object. Critics of Plato have either misunderstood Plato's claim (thinking that he was identifying love and desire) or misunderstood the nature of desire (thinking that desire is egocentric). The fourth issue, the connection of love and valuation, has in modern times been debated as an issue between *eros* and *agape*. My main concern has been to define this issue, which has never been properly understood. I argue that it has nothing to do with the supposed egocentricity of *eros* versus the supposed selflessness of *agape.* The real distinction is between two attitudes toward values: whether value-properties exist objectively, independently of human decisions or attitudes or feeling, as in the classical, Platonic conception of the world; or whether they are relative to human or divine conventions or attitudes or feelings. A second conception of *eros* and *agape* is also of importance, however, and concerns the causal priority of beliefs or feelings in bringing about the attitude of love.*

J A B

* I am grateful to Ann Brentlinger and Alex Page for helpful criticisms of earlier drafts of this essay.